P9-DJA-429

Early Promise, Late Reward

A Biography of Helen Hooven Santmyer

Author of "…And Ladies of the Club."

By Joyce C. Quay

Contents

Preface

"I believe that order is better than chaos, creation better than destruction. I prefer gentleness to violence, forgiveness to vendetta. On the whole I think knowledge is preferable to ignorance, and I am sure that human sympathy is more valuable than ideology. I believe that in spite of the recent triumphs of science, men haven't changed much in the last two thousand years; and in consequence we must still try to learn from history. ...I believe in courtesy, the ritual by which we avoid hurting other people's feelings by satisfying our own egos."

Kenneth Clark wrote those words in his well known book, *Civilization* (Harper & Row, Publishers, 1969).

Helen Hooven Santmyer applauded his sentiments.

Acknowledgements

Mrs. Caroline Westmore

Mrs. Jane Wiliamson

Weldon Kefauver

The Ohio State University Press

The Ohio State University Library -- Rare Books Room

Wellesley College Archives and Alumnae Office

Cedarville College Administration Office

Dayton Public Library

Xenia Public Library -- Geneology Room

Greene County Historical Society

MacDowell Colony

Oscar Collier & Associates

Special thanks to Rita McCullough and Sandy Brown

Dedication

To John Grier Quay
without whose support and understanding
this book would not have been written.

Ohio Commission on Aging Honors
Helen Hooven Santmyer

∝✺↩

"...Her accomplishment stands as an
inspiration to all who would follow
their own special star."

List of Illustrations

Helen Hooven Santmyer, circa 1900

Helen's graduation picture from Wellesley College (1918)

Helen (for winning Ohioana Award), 1982

Geneology

❧

HOOVEN

Diederich Schenck - b. 1485
m
Anna Yanberlaer

Peter Schenck - b. 1547 d.?
m
Maria Yanberlaer

Martin Schenck - b. 1584 emigrated 1650
m
?

Roelof Schenck - b. 1619 emigrated 1650
m
Neeltje G. Vancouvenhoven

Jan Roeldese Schenck - b. 1670 d.?
m
Sarah Vancouvenhoven (1st cousin)

John Schenck - b .6-27-1722 d. 12-24-1808
m
Neltje Bennet

John Schenck - b. 1752 d.?
m
Rhoda Holmes

John Holmes Schenk - b. 8-26-1779 d. 1870
m
Sarah Lane - b. 1783 (NJ) d. 1820

Continued

Annaletta Schenck - b. 1820   d. 1890
m
John Mathias Catrow - b. 3-15-1813   d.?

Sarah Amanda Catrow - b. 1-27-1842   d. 1919
m
Enoch Patterson Hooven - b. 6-12-1842   d. 1919

Bertha Hooven - b. 9-17-1868   d. 4-1955
m
Joseph Wright Santmyer - b. 5-7-1870   d. 10-1954

Helen Hooven Santmyer	Jane	Philip Hooven
b. 11-25-1895 d. 1986	b. 1897 d. 1992	b. 11-18-1908 d.?
	m	
	Fred Anderson	

Martha Jane (Jane)	Caroline (Terry)	Daniel Erwin
m	*m*	*m*
John Williamson	Edward Westbrook	Virginia Dolber

∽⨾∾

SANTMYER

Captain John Marcellus Santmyer - b. 1790 (Insbruck)   d. 1853
m
Mary Elder

Charles Augustus Santmyer - b. 4-29-1839   d. 1921
m
Helen Marie Wright

Joseph Wright Santmyer - b. 5-7-1870   d. October 1954
m
Bertha Hooven - b. 9-17-1868   d. April 1955

Helen Hooven Santmyer	Jane	Philip Hooven
b. 11-25-1895 d. 1986	b. 1897 d. 1992	b. 11-18-1908 d.?

Introduction

In 1984 literary history was made by a little old lady from Xenia, Ohio when Helen Hooven Santmyer's novel, "...*And Ladies of the Club*"[1] became a best seller. On the eve of her 100th birthday (1995) it is time to review her success and to realize that Helen's life is a prime example for all of us. We must each follow our "special star."

The *New York Times* front page on January 12, 1984, proclaimed, "Happy End for Novelist's 50-year Effort." "Her Dream Comes True...at the Age of 88," headlined the *Boston Globe*. "Too bad it [fame] didn't happen to her at a younger age," said some. Others suggested, as did Helen, "It wouldn't have made such a sensation if it had."

Helen had considered herself to be a writer since she was ten years old. For many years she worked under what she considered the most trying circumstances and made great sacrifices, including the opportunity for a husband and family. It would be ironic, indeed, if her fame and fortune were based on the fact that she was still able to write when she was eighty eight years old.

It is true that a bestseller written by an octogenarian is unusual, but her popularity was not based on her age alone. Since her spectacular success in 1984, two novels *Herbs and Apples*[2] and *Fierce Dispute*,[3] written in her youth and published in the 1920s have been reissued; *Ohio Town*,[4] a collection of her short pieces on Xenia, has continued to sell very well; and a previously unpublished novel, *Farewell Summer*,[5] was well received.

"Why should I read some old woman's book about a ladies' club in a small Ohio town?" Many people asked that question when Helen Hooven Santmyer's book, "...*And Ladies of the Club*," was first published in 1982; many people might ask the same question ten years later. Perhaps Helen explained it best herself when she said of her books, "...they show what life was like when people relied on themselves -- when they had principles."

In writing about her time and place she has left us a more positive picture of the Midwest than those painted by Sinclair Lewis in *Main Street*[6] and Sherwood Anderson in *Winesburg Ohio*,[7] which have been used in American Literature courses for decades. All three writers were anxious to break away from their roots and gain their independence in the big city, but Helen seems to be the one who appreciated the importance of her roots and looked back with a realization of how fortunate she had been to have them.

Helen wrote about the late 19th Century and the early 20th, still referred to as the Victorian era. The January 16, 1988, issue of *Newsweek* proclaimed: "Victoriana Rules Again. Americans re-discover frills and furbelows -- fashions and family life, circa 1885." About the same time a new magazine called *Victoria* appeared on the stands, dedicated solely to the return of tradition and graciousness. Among the letters of praise to the editors many came from young readers 13 to 18. "Let us never let that golden age of grace be forgotten... First off, I am 15 years old... [discovering the past] I felt as if I'd found something I'd been looking for all my life."

That is Helen's kind of reader!

For all of this Helen struggled with traditions and fought for her independence. She left home, determined to make it on her own. She may have leaned too far in that direction, however, for many who came in contact with her described her as "distant," "different," "unfriendly," "strange," and some of her students claimed she was "a perfectionist" who demanded perfection from them. She smoked and liked cocktails which was not acceptable behavior in a small Ohio town in the early 20th Century, and she seemed to have abandoned the traditions with which she was raised. All of these things made her suspect in that world.

On the other hand, her writings advocated family, manners, church, gracious living, and above all, tradition. They represented the "internals" Helen wrote about and are the things that draw us to her. Her rebellion and fight for independence were the externals she showed the world.

While planning a trip to Xenia to visit my aunt, I called from my home in Connecticut and made an appointment to see Helen in the nursing home during my stay. Something about "...And Ladies of the Club" had struck a chord in me, spoke to my Midwestern background. Although I visited her several times I was never prepared for the sight of that frail little woman, suffering from emphysema, lying on the bed with oxygen tanks nearby. It belied the glint in her eyes and her smile.

People with whom I have talked about Helen would deny she ever smiled but to me she was always cordial, seemed glad to see me, and smiled. Perhaps because we shared so many things, she felt I was a kindred spirit. I had my roots in Greene County. My ancestors, too, had helped settle the territory. I had gone to college in Boston, worked in New York City when a young girl, loved England, lived in California the same years she did. Mostly, we shared a love of Ohio and always returned to our roots no matter how far away life took us. At that time, however, I had no thought of writing her biography so our visits were purely social.

In researching Helen's life and interviewing the few people still around who knew her, I found she was not popular with her peers. Even her family members were not very fond of her. I found her candor refreshing, her manner cordial. We established an instant rapport. Helen was not only the hard, indifferent person she showed the world, she was also the warm caring person that she thought herself to be. Of course, I was not a sibling and I didn't have to cope with what seemed to be laziness while doing her chores for her.

Finding her to be an interesting person who had a message to impart on the importance of our historic values, I realized I wanted to write about Helen Hooven Santmyer and share her message with others. Research for this biography has been compiled from Helen's papers and manuscripts held by The Ohio State University and her own books which are somewhat autobiographical. In addition, there is a family genealogy compiled by a relative, and I have conducted interviews with her surviving family members, former students, townspeople including her landlord in Cedarville and the former mayor of Xenia as well as people with whom she worked. The greatest contribution, however, is from Helen herself in the form of five hundred personal letters written to her family from Wellesley, Oxford and New York City. All of these things help to put flesh on the frail old woman and show her as a three-dimensional person.

It is my premise that Helen lived much of her life in her writing. There are many details about conversations and feelings that cannot be verified. The people who knew are gone, and I must rely on what she told me in our conversations and my own experiences to fill in some of the blanks. I have written a book which might explain some of the "whys" of her behavior and give readers cause to consider their own special stars in their own time and place.

Not until Helen was dead and I was researching her papers in The Ohio State University library did I find her childhood diary, written when she was 11 years old. In it she had stated, "When I am famous someone will want to write my life. I hope it will be done before I die. I would like to read it -- they can write about my death in an appendix afterward."[8]

My apologies to Helen for being so late.

Part I

(1895-1918)

Reflections

❧

Chapter 1

❦

The Return

Helen, returning on the train to Xenia fresh from Wellesley College graduation, looked at her reflection in the train window while contemplating her passing youth and her future.

The words of the commencement speaker still echoed in her mind. "The great need of the hour is spiritual courage born of high spirited idealism. Courage and idealism, let it be remembered, always go together." Dr. Raymond Calkins, Pastor of the First Congregational Church of Cambridge, Massachusetts had been selected as commencement speaker to the class of 1918, perhaps because he was the brother of Mary White Calkins, Wellesley's professor of Psychology and Philosophy. To the wartime graduating class, his words had meaning and gave the girls a sense of purpose. "...we need the idealism which not only lays bare the ultimate causes of the collapse of our civilization, but clearly perceives the spiritual bases on which it must be rebuilt. To you belongs this high duty of giving moral direction, as it were, to the whole body of public opinion."[1]

As Helen had always known she would be a writer, she now knew the direction her writing must take -- making people see the value in a structured society which had rules and standards. Only when people know what is expected of them can civilization continue. The click of the train riding over the rails seemed to repeat the words.

Train number Twenty-One[2] from Pennsylvania Station in New York City to points South and West -- Philadelphia, Washington, D.C., Harrisburg, Pittsburg, Columbus -- had as distinct a personality as any famous trans-Atlantic liner. Twenty-One left Penn Station in the afternoon and arrived in Xenia, Ohio early the following morning. "...it was the favorite coming-home train of our part of the world. It brought us back from college for our holidays, and from New York in the days before that city was within easy motoring distance,"[3] Helen Santmyer wrote.

This day Twenty-One was bringing Helen home. Mother, Father and her sister, Jane, who had just finished her sophomore year at Wellesley, were travelling with Helen, but she was alone with her thoughts. She was coming home to Ohio, to Xenia and to Greene County, the land of her ancestors. Home!

As children, Helen and Jane had often played the game of Experienced Traveler. They probably only traveled as far as Columbus or Cincinnati on the day coach, but while waiting in the depot no one would know how far they were going. Acting blase` and indifferent, the two young girls imparted something like contempt for their fellow travelers. Taking their places next to the windows, Helen and Jane would press their noses to the sooty glass, careful not to put their elbows or gloved hands on the grimy window sills, and Helen would retreat to play "in the delightful privacy of the mind."[4]

She would pretend she was coming home after years of absence, rich and famous, as heads turned with envy. "Of course," Helen wrote years later, "you were not, in your mind's eye, coming home in the day coach, but in the most august of Pullmans; you were rich, which was of minor importance, and famous, which was very important indeed. People recognized you and stared; when the train slowed and the porter came for your bags, they wondered audibly: Why should she be getting off here, in this funny little town?"[5]

In *Ohio Town*, Helen writes that Noah was the porter on train Twenty-One. Noah had watched Helen mature from a tomboy to a young lady of fashion. How pleasant it was to be recognized by him "...first as a child in our own station, then later as an adult in the Pennsylvania Station in New York." Noah had known Helen all of her life and had watched as she and Jane grew up. He must have commented with pride on her graduation from that fine Eastern college. Not many girls from Xenia did that. His own daughter would go to college at Wilberforce University just a few miles north of Xenia. How long did she plan to be at home? What did she plan to do?

Through the night the train covered the rails south to Washington D.C., then west through Pennsylvania. "Before the train reached the station," Helen tells us in *Herbs and Apples*, "the country flattened out and became a wide panorama of undulating hills..." This was Helen's country and she knew every hill and bend in the road. Somehow, even the air was fresher here, the sky bluer. Every mile the train traveled was a mile closer to home.

During those train rides long ago, Helen's childhood dreams took many forms, but they all had one thing in common. They all covered so much ground so rapidly that all "desirable ends"[6] were attained by the age of twenty-five, leaving the other two thirds of life a complete blank. Each dream was different but fame was achieved in every one. Only when she stumbled off the day coach to the brick pavement of her own station would Helen face reality. On this June day in 1918, when the train arrived at the Xenia depot, Helen was jerked back once more from her reveries to the here-and-now. The station platform, she told us in *Ohio Town*, "was a paved brick area (shaped like a flattened triangle) with the freight depot in one acute angle, the passenger station (with its baggage rooms, express office and restaurant) in the other angle at the far end. The space between the two buildings was paved with old worn sun-baked bricks"[7]...a welcoming sight.

Helen gave us so much detail and description because she wanted us to understand how important the railroad was to the life of the community then. People complained about the noise and the dirty trains, but being able to travel on them was a privilege and, many times, a necessity. Almost all produce came into the town via train in those days; cars were not very reliable for long distances so most people -- those who were able to afford it -- depended on the trains for travel. The depot was the hub of commerce. In the days of World War I, as during the Civil War fifty-some years before, the station was a bedlam of activity: train dispatchers, railroad crews, uniformed soldiers and passengers hurrying to and fro.

Helen had imagined a triumphant return with a welcoming home at the station before she was twenty-five, but this wartime activity was not what she had in mind. Amid the hubbub, Helen was not aware of the heads that turned and regarded her with admiration as the slender young woman, nattily dressed in the latest fashion, followed her father to the waiting room and carriage.

Miss Toohey, like Noah, was an institution on the Pennsylvania Railroad. She was in charge of the ladies waiting room in the depot, making Xenia known as the best on the line. She too had known Helen since childhood and watched Miss Santmyer mature from a tomboy to a young lady of fashion. Miss Toohey had a "grandmotherly air," Helen wrote in *Ohio Town*. "You could see at a glance that she was kind, capable, and would stand for no nonsense...Her sandy hair (which faded into silver as the years passed) was parted in the middle, plaited and twisted into a flat bun on the back of her head. Her dresses were black with long full skirts. She always wore a white apron...with ruffles and wide starched strings."[8]

Miss Toohey would have noticed the chic traveling suit Miss Santmyer wore. She must have noticed that it came from Boston because Xenia's finest, Huchison and Gibney's on Main Street, had nothing like it. She must have wondered, too, what Miss Santmyer would do with her life now.

When the baggage was collected the waiting carriage took them the long way around to the house on Third Street. Father had arranged for a quick turn around the courthouse square to show Helen that the town hadn't changed much in four years even if she had.

Helen had often written of the town and this courthouse in her papers, themes and exams at college. They said to write about what you know and Helen knew Xenia. She had made these buildings and this countryside a reality for those who had never seen them. She made the people come alive when she wrote sketches of its citizens. By the time she left Wellesley most of her friends felt they had shared a piece of Helen's home.

As an example, consider the clock in the courthouse tower. Coming into town from any direction, one could see the four-faced clock. It was an essential part of the lives of the people of the town -- consulting it on daily walks to town, listening for the slow chime in pace with their lives. Her friends at Wellesley knew the story of the time Helen went to a party in the country. The hours passed quickly then someone realized it had gotten quite late. They made a mad dash for home -- midnight was the deadline. The light in the clock went out at midnight, and the young people held their breath as the carriage raced to the center of town. Was the light out? Were they in trouble? As they rounded the curve and saw the tower in the distance, they shouted. The clock was still shining brightly and they were safe, this time. The host's clock, it seems, was fast and they easily beat the curfew. Helen always wondered, was that accidental or intentional on the part of the host? Seeing the old clock, Helen recalled that night as the driver of the Santmyer carriage began to hurry to the house on Third Street. Grandmother was waiting for them.

The old house had been built by Helen's grandparents after the Civil War. When Helen was five years old, she moved with her parents from Cincinnati to join her grandmother and grandfather in the large white house that still welcomed them. She had grown up here and the sight never failed to give her a warm feeling.

"To the right of the steps a gate in the iron fence gave entrance to the side yard; once beyond the hedge and shrubbery that lined the fence you could see, beneath the high branches of the great black-boughed tulip trees, a wide stretch of lawn, ending in a green lattice, and beyond the lattice, the tops of the fruit trees; you could see the side of the house that looked out on the cool shadows and into the boughs of the trees, the set-in porch, with vine-covered railing upstairs and the slim white pillars ·and the small, fan-shaped terrace that extended from the porch to the lawn. Around this terrace there was a retaining wall of brick, and on that a low iron fence, both wall and fence were smothered in honeysuckle.

"A path descended from the terrace by three brick steps and crossed to the opposite side of the lawn, where, beneath the trees, stood a moldy fountain: a moss-grown fawn playing in the silvery water. A fountain, where the birds splashed and shadows of the leaves quivered on the pool, and the sun made rainbows..."[9]

Helen's life would undergo many changes before she gained the fame to warrant a brass plaque on the front door of her house, but the train ride home from Boston after graduation gave Helen a chance to reflect on her young life. Dr. Calkins had spoken about the young women going into the world -- looking ahead. Before she could look ahead, Helen felt she needed some time to think about where she had come from and who she was. Then she would consider who she would become.

Chapter 2

❧

The Growing Years

Helen was born in Cincinnati, Ohio on November 25, 1895. It was in Cincinnati that her parents, Bertha Hooven and Joseph Santmyer, met at the University of Cincinnati where Bertha studied fine arts and Joseph was a medical student. The trauma of delivering a baby who died, however, caused Joseph to rethink his career path. Talking over his future with his family, he realized the field of business was probably best for him. Bertha's family owned a rope making company in Xenia, and they offered him a position, but Joseph thought it wiser not to work for his father-in-law. He turned the offer down and instead accepted one from R.A. Kelly Company, a competitor in Xenia.

Helen was always disapointed that her father had not continued in his career as a doctor. Somehow, she felt, it was more presitgious to be a doctor than to have a career in business. Mr. Santmyer, however, was happy in his job as Secretary-Treasurer of a manufacturer of cordage and machinery, and he proved to be a good provider.

Joseph and Bertha moved their young family (Helen was five years old and her sister Jane was three) to the large Hooven family home at

113 South Third Street. The house was large enough to hold three generations with ease and, in those days of extended family, it was not an unusual thing to do. It was this house, described in the previous chapter, which would represent home to Helen for the rest of her life.

When Helen was ten years old she began to keep a diary. It was not a fancy one with a lock and key, but a simple mottle-covered blank composition book like the ones they used in school. She wrote in it with a stubby pencil -- VERY neatly -- as if for posterity. This diary was a record of her observations and the events that touched her young life.

Helen knew she wanted to be a writer when she was very young, and she set about the task of learning her craft. A writer needed to observe everything and impart those observations to others. "...this diary would someday be a cherished possession of my biographer, or my great great grandchild would find the yellowed paper in the attic, and it would reveal to an eager world the early writings of the famous and beloved Helen Santmyer." And, " When I am famous someone will want to write my Life; I hope it can be done before I die. I would like to read it -- they can write about my death in an appendix afterward." Helen was a very forward thinking little girl.

She adopted the idea of keeping a diary from Lousia May Alcott, her role-model, who kept journals all her life. Helen described her first little diary in *Herbs and Apples*: "There is never a child who does not fancy himself the subject of a biography, and [with] nine hundred and ninety-nine out of a thousand nothing is achieved (by the person) but a line on a tombstone. Biographies are inadequate for the few who are worth it, anyway, for no one can possibly know what are the important things -- the 'internals' of one's life."[1]

In 1907 and 1908, when she was eleven and twelve in the sixth and seventh grades, her diary was her attempt to let her future biographers see those "internals." Helen expected to be famous and the famous, she thought, were always subjects of biographies. She intended to help her biographer all she could.

The desire to become a writer took form on the day Helen discovered Louisa May Alcott. She recorded in her diary on April 22, 1907, "My time for hero worship has begun. Mine are Miss Harper [her teacher] and Miss Alcott...I got a life of Miss Alcott from the library, and I think it is VERY good. I like Louisa Alcott, I finished it, but I want to copy *My Beth* and a letter of L.A.'s in as near her handwriting as I can."[2]

To emulate Louisa in every way was Helen's goal. She saw herself as the devoted daughter, caring for Mama and Papa someday, and giving up her life to take care of her sister. In reality, Helen was absorbed in her own work and dreams and was often reluctant to be interrupted. Her frail health may have contributed to her parents' tolerance of this behavior, but her siblings remember her as shunning daily chores which they had to do in her place. They didn't see her as one who would take care of anyone.

The diary was her confidante -- she could be herself and no pose was required. Helen was no stranger to poses. She adopted a pose when she rode the day coach to Cincinnati as in later years she would adopt many poses as a defense. In the forward of *Herbs and Apples*, she describes Derrick [her alter-ego] as having "built defenses early"... she was "inscrutable and imperturbable."[3] This description of Derrick would be applied to Helen many times by many people.

A revelation had come to Helen while reading the last pages of *The Life and Journals of Louisa May Alcott*.[4] "The veil had been lifted," and Helen knew she would be a great writer when she grew up. If you want to be a writer, she thought, you have to sit down and write. She wrote all kinds of things. Helen did not leave us a copy of an early book, written when she was twelve and entitled *The Trials and Tribulations of the McCarthy Family*, but in her diary she does describe a play she wrote in 1908. She called it *The Titled Twelve*, and we do know that it contained six chapters: The Newcomers, School and Schoolmates, Surprises, The Party, Two Suggestions, and Two Surprises Carried Out. It covered twenty-four handwritten pages and was illustrated by two drawings.

Helen also published a newspaper that same year. She was already a prolific writer. It was called *The Xenian Weekly Eagle*, and cost two dollars a month to subscribe. Considering the fact that a major daily newspaper usually cost three cents a day, it is apparent Helen put a high price on her work.

There was society news:

Tues. Sept 8, 1907

Mr. Clark McKay is enjoying a visit at West Virginia. He will resume his music teaching Sept. 9. Miss Charlie Santmyer [Helen's cousin] left for Cincinnati Sunday where she will stay with relatives until Wed. From there she will go to Virginia.

Miss Florence Ankeney is staying at Flynn's during the teacher's Institute. The Mabons are the guests of Mr. and Mrs. Moorehead. Mr. and Mrs. Prugh entertained for Miss Gertrude Mower and her bridal party. Miss Florence Steele has been quite ill since her trip to Canada.

There were also editorials in *The Xenian Weekly Eagle*:

School Question

The Xenia Public Schools are not perfect, at least in my opinion. There being only six McGuffey's Readers, they are stretched from the fourth to the eighth grade. The fourth reader is read in the fourth and fifth grades, the fifth in the fifth and sixth grades, and the sixth in the eighth. If we had a little more Grammar, Composition and History and not so much arithmetic we would be better off. Some

teachers are too easy on us and some are too strict.
Miss Harper is a good teacher. (H.S.)

Frequently, Helen's little newspaper did seem to be editorially biased. It might interest the reader to know, for example, that Helen was very good at grammar, composition and history, but she was not particularly good at arithmetic.

Like all newspapers *The Xenian Weekly Eagle* had a staff of reporters. One M.F. turned in this copy:

August Tue 27, 1907
My Visit To Sulpher Lick

The next morning I got up and took a walk. I walked way past Maple Grove. When I came home it was breakfast time. After breakfast I went out and played. We had a fine dinner. After dinner Mary Crow and I walked down to the [railroad] station. After we came home I taught Mary how to dance. In the evening when the people would dance, we would dance with them. The next morning all the people were making souvenir canes they made Mary and I a cane.

The spelling wasn't very good, nor was the grammar but it was all their own work.

In 1908 Helen entered the eighth grade in Xenia High School, the big rectangular brick building with the four-story tower in the center. It would be torn down in 1922 to make room for a modern one; there Helen would be teacher, not student. For the next four years, however, Helen would shine as one of the school's prized students, and it was there that memories would be made.

When she started her freshman year she also started a scrapbook, 1908-1912. On the flyleaf she wrote in a clear hand:

Memory Book
of H. Santmyer

"While the heartbeat's young - O the splendor of the spring,
With all her dewy jewels on, is not so fair a thing"

The joys of youth are fleeting, Helen believed, and she added, "I only mark the hours that shine."

The Memory Book opens with the words, "When We Were Freshmen." What does one put into a Memory Book? Helen's memories are preserved with carefully chosen pictures, some hand-drawn, as well as limericks and poems to commemorate events. Christmas cards and New Years cards from favorite teachers like the one Miss Irma Finley sent her:

"All happiness attend thee, May each New Year better and richer find thee,

Lovingly, Irma Finley."

Helen also collected leaves in her Memory Book. One was gathered during the freshman class picnic; one from Victoria's Monument in Richmond, Virginia; another from the Old Church Tower in Jamestown; one from the tree planted by General Lafayette in Yorktown; and still another from Lord Cornwallis' Headquarters in Yorktown. The leaves from Virginia were gathered during her summer vacation in 1910 while Helen was visiting her aunt and uncle in Claremont. That vacation was particularly notable because it was the start of what would become a life-long correspondence with her parents in which she would hone her descriptive skills in writing about people and places.

Helen's family always made a point of passing on bits of family gossip and local news to her. In the summer of 1910, there was a GAR Encampment, sponsored by the veterans of the Grand Army of the Republic who survived this country's Civil War. Xenia's streets were filled with parades and tents and many strangers, Mrs. Santmyer wrote to her daughter. There was a merry-go-round, side shows and even a fat lady's tent on the corner of their street. She, for one, would be glad when the whole thing was over, but Helen's grandfather was enjoying himself immensely. Mrs. Santmyer promised to send the clipping from the *Xenia Gazette* to Grandpa Santmyer in Virginia so Helen could read all about it.

Helen's Grandfather Hooven, a veteran of that conflict, often told the family of his experiences, and he enjoyed reminiscing with his old friends during the Encampment. Helen's father, writing to tell her about the town's events, suggested Helen ask her Grandfather Santmyer [who was also a Civil War veteran] to tell her about his war experiences while she was visiting. The memories and stories related by those two old men would provide the basis for parts of *Ohio Town* as well as the Civil War years in Helen's best selling novel, *"...And Ladies of the Club"* many years later.

Those early letters from her father were a preview of the many he would write during the years she was away at college and in Europe, offering fatherly advice and encouragement and assuring Helen he was always at hand if she needed him. He also reported that the family was well and hoped she was in good health. In his letter of June 15, 1910, he closed as he would many times in future letters, "I hope you will continue to enjoy yourself. Let me know if you are short of money."

Helen's mother was concerned about Helen's clothing. Did she have enough? Did she need anything? "Keep your clothes in good condition," she advised Helen, "and be very good and sweet." Helen was trying to be good, she wrote, and she was having a marvelous time visiting with her relatives. In addition to visits to Yorktown, Jamestown and Richmond, they had traveled to Newport News to see the launching of a new steamship.

Before the visit ended, Father enclosed in his letter a "draft" to cover any expenses Helen might have and to buy her railroad ticket for the trip home. "Ask Aunt Jane to write me what her plans are for starting you home," he suggested.

"Dear Oppie," Helen replied, reverting to her childhood nickname for her father, "I received your letter and check safely and will now tell you all the plans." Having related all the details of the trip home, Helen added a postscript. "Aunt Jessie says she doesn't think she needs to write, and she says you can rely on my statements. I assure you they are perfectly authentic." Fathers, it seems, seldom realize how grown-up their daughters have become.

Helen returned and the vacation was over. Sophomore year in the Memory Book began with tickets from high school football games (priced at fifteen cents) and birthday party invitations. It included a handbill announcing the opening of Greene County's new Young Women's Christian Association -- that was important to Helen, who was among the first to join. The First Reformed Presbyterian Church, which the Santmyers had attended for many years, dedicated a new beautiful stone building with large stained glass windows. Helen included the dedication program in her memory book and wrote about the church later in *Herbs and Apples* and *Ohio Town*.

As a heading to mark her Junior year, Helen wrote [paraphrasing Alexander Pope] "A little knowledge is a dangerous thing -- Drink deep or taste not of the Pierian springs." She would make that a guideline for her life and one could say she never stopped learning.

But it wasn't all books for Helen. She was a sociable person, and there would be more than educational pursuits to interest her. That year in her Memory Book she added "at home" invitations, a clever handmade Halloween party invitation, tickets from the spring baseball games and evidence that Helen played softball herself. She was a lifelong baseball fan. There was also a pressed rose. We can only guess its significance. Was it from Fredrick or William, the two names that showed up more than once in Helen's memories?

For many of the treasures she committed to the Memory Book there were limericks and poems to reflect her feelings connected with them. Even while she was in high school, Helen had an avid interest in the political affairs of the country and her community. In 1911 she wrote,

"Small poets, small musicians; small painters, and still smaller politicians." Although always a staunch Republican, she never changed her opinion of politicians.

Signaling the end of the school year, a production of *The Vicar of Wakefield* was offered by Xenia High School's Junior Class in the spring of 1912. Helen did not have the lead role, but she was in the cast and she worked for the Dramatic Club as she would later at Wellesley College. There are pictures of her classmates on the last pages of that junior year and then -- in large printed letters -- "SENIORS AT LAST; EXIT CHILDHOOD..." followed by a drawing of a little girl with her head cast down, reluctantly walking away.

The senior year at Xenia was one of hard work and concern over entrance exams for Wellesley. It had been decided very early that Wellesley College was appropriate for Helen because so many friends and family members had gone there. All her teachers encouraged her. They knew she would qualify. She had always been a good student and everyone expected great things from her. But Helen was never over-confident and even with her scholastic record she was concerned that she might not be accepted. During her four years of preparation at Xenia High, Helen studied: four years of English, four years of Latin, American History, Botany, Modern History, Chemistry, Algebra, Plane Geometry, Solid Geometry, Physiology and two years of German.

Before graduation, however, there were many parties, picnics, ball games and dances. It was an exciting time, and the summer was still ahead before leaving for college in the East. Helen, of course, had been away from home before, but this time it seemed different and more permanent. With mixed feelings she prepared to leave the security of her home and family and Xenia, Ohio -- her town. When the letter of acceptance arrived from Wellesley, Helen, who could always rise to the occasion, entered into the new adventure with enthusiasm.

Chapter 3

❧

Wellesley's Ivied Halls

Most of us have one place, one time that was a high point in our lives. It could have been high school, boarding school, college, first job. Whatever it was--all other times are measured against that point. So it was with Helen Santmyer. Wellesley was the apex of her life. From those four years she would judge every other experience.

On the Pullman from Xenia to Boston, Helen met friends of her Xenia friends who attended Wellesley, resulting in lots of fun and lots of advice. When the girl from Xenia arrived on the Wellesley campus on the afternoon of September 15, 1914, she threw herself immediately into the social life of the college as well as the sports and her studies. She wanted to be involved in everything. Her early letters fairly bubbled with enthusiasm and joy. Even small things -- a "spread" or a concert or a group of friends getting together to talk -- were exciting and, usually, "the best I ever had."[1]

She immediately felt she had the best dorm, the best floor with the best girls. On the second floor of The Eliot, twenty nine girls shared two bathrooms, but there was never the slightest hint of complaint about the inconvenience. Determined to keep close ties with home, Helen was committed to telling her family every detail of her life at Wellesley.

To show where The Eliot, her dormitory, was located in relationship to the other buildings, her first letter included her hand-drawn map of the campus "with its lawn as smooth as velvet and so green." Helen described the lake, seen on her walk around the campus that first day -- "as blue as the sky and so smooth it reflects everything." College buildings were on one side of the lake and "on the opposite shore is an 'almost mountain' that is covered with trees." Her walk also included the still-standing ruins of College Hall, which had burned before Helen arrived, and the beautiful white stone buildings that housed the art department and the library. Helen described the beauty of Wellesley's classic brick buildings covered with ivy; she also commented on the "new building," which, according to Helen, no one liked. The construction of the "new building" was Victorian at its worst, Helen thought, too much ornate wood trim on the outside and too many dark ornate carvings on the interior.

In one of her first letters, she included a map of her second floor living quarters at Eliot. Each room was labeled and included occupants' names and brief biographies. In addition, she drew a sketch of the room plan -- where the furniture was located, whose bed was whose, etc. She laid the ground work so that her parents would be able to relate to her physical surroundings through the days and years to come.

The campus was only four blocks from the village of Wellesley, referred to as the Vil. "There are only three business blocks," Helen wrote, "the rest is residential." She thought the town was beautiful, "wide streets and old, old trees, beautiful homes all with wide lawns." It was in this village that the girls bought their necessities and food, posted their mail, frequented the Tea Room and on special occasions were treated to a meal at the Wellesley Inn. Helen commented to her parents, "a few professors [who live in the village] must be rich...they are always running around in their little "electrics" [cars]."

Helen's roommate, Elinor Todd, she described as, "...not just the one I would pick, [however] she is awfully jolly and nice. But you should see her clothes! Mercy! They fill her closet to overflowing." To her delight, she was to find that Eli was as serious a student as Helen herself.

When her parents read about Elinor's clothes, they quickly wrote to ask Helen if she had enough clothes and were they appropriate. Helen assured them that she had an adaquate wardrobe and they need not worry, "they're as good as most and better than some."

When she was a child, Helen was considered a tomboy. Her mother always made bloomers to match her dresses for one never knew when Helen would fall in the pond or follow the boys climbing trees. It was said she had climbed every tree in Xenia.

Since she had given up her tomboy ways, Helen had taken an interest in clothes and fashion and frequently informed her mother and Jane of the newest fashions in the East. She would draw sketches of her latest fashionable hair style and the design of the latest dress she had bought or made. She was surprised to learn that smocks had not yet become the fashion in Xenia. They were all the rage at Wellesley; she herself had just gotten a new pink one -- to be worn with a belt. She would find a pattern to send home so that Mother could make one for Jane. "Would Jane have the nerve to wear it," Helen wondered.

"We 'got off the board walk' for the funniest faculty you ever saw," said Helen, using contemporary vernacular. "I could hardly get over it. I told the girls we didn't raise 'em in Ohio like that. But we do. -- Mrs....is a specimen." Helen would frequently soften an originally harsh judgment about people or places. "I've learned this about Wellesley faculty -- the handsome, well-dressed ones are mere unimportant instructors and all the wise and re-knowned ones are frumps." Again, she softened her criticism, "Except Miss Pendleton, who dresses beautifully..."

Helen also regaled her family with every detail of her culinary experiences. We know, for instance, that her first breakfast at Wellesley consisted of corn flakes or cream of wheat, toast, egg, coffee or cocoa. For lunch they were served cheese and potato mixture, macaroni and tomatoes cooked together, hot rolls, milk and baked apples. Dinner consisted of sliced veal, sweet potatoes and chocolate ice cream. "So you see, they are mostly things I like."

Having included descriptions of activities and traditions for freshmen to the extent that she had experienced them, that first letter to home ended with, "I'm not one bit homesick, but simply crazy about it all."

Every letter home opened with a version of "I'm sorry I haven't written sooner but..." The letters continued to describe food of every kind. Of a surprise party for her roommate Eli, she wrote, "The room was full of people, including two seniors, and loads to eat -- animal crackers, crackers and jelly, crackers and peanut butter, sweet pickles, sour pickles [always a favorite of Helen's], olives, cheese crackers, crackerjack, apples and grapes and a pie." Thus Helen described the menu of the first of-many "spreads."

The first afternoon reception she attended included raspberry ice cream and ladyfingers. Helen commented that one of her friends had "pull" because they had four ladyfingers apiece. The reception was crowded and the girls kept bumping into each other, "...but it didn't lesson our joy." Through the years, especially when she was in Europe and became so ill that she was put on a very limited diet, she would remember the food and the parties so important to the students then.

It is interesting to note the value of money in those years during and immediately after The Great War. Why, for instance did a student at Wellesley, Massachusetts send her dirty clothes to Xenia, Ohio to be washed? Because, sent by Railway Express at laundry rate, it cost only two and a half cents a pound, or thirty-five cents. Stamps for all letters cost two cents, and in those days Helen could send a letter to Ohio and expect a response within a week.

Then, too, when a Wellesley woman went into Boston to shop for a new dress, she could expect to find a nice dress, originally priced at twenty-eight dollars, marked down to fifteen dollars. On that same trip to town, one could go to the Copely Theater and see a legitimate play for twenty-five cents if one sat in the second balcony which Helen assured her parents were wonderful seats. Also, by utilizing "rush seats" at the symphony, one could hear performers like Fritz Kreisler for as little as thirty-five cents. They were called "rush seats" because the people in line who did not have tickets were allowed to rush up the stairs and grab a seat as long as they were available. Also, at the opera house one could hear Dame Nellie Melba or Galli Curci for a similar low price.

When Wellesley women went into Boston to eat, or even into the village for tea, the cost would only be a few cents. One could have tea and cookies in the restaurant atop Filene's Department Store for ten cents...that even included tea dancing. Helen received twenty-five dollars each month from her father. That allowed her to buy necessities, entertain at tea, enjoy good entertainment in Boston, and provide presents for family members.

Only once did Helen ever ask for additional funds and that was during her senior year when she had unaccustomed expenses for commencement. Again concerned, Helen's parents asked if her allowance was adequate. Helen replied that she had ample for her needs and that none of the women spent very much. Economizing was fashionable.

Once Helen had adjusted to new friends, a strenuous academic schedule, and organized activities like sports, the Ohio Club and the Christian Association, she was faced with the coming holidays. Unable to go home, perhaps because of time and financial restrictions, she spent that first Thanksgiving and Christmas -- her first away from home -- with a dozen or so left on campus. "We are going to have a glorious time alright." For members of the Greek class, Miss Harcum gave a tea on Wednesday before the holiday. "...awfully nice even if all we did was drink tea and knit." Wednesday night a friend who lived in a private house invited them over to make candy and enjoy an enormous "spread" provided by boxes received from the mothers of friends.

Thanksgiving Day dinner at the college was a traditional feast, Helen related to her family later. There were even place cards. The diners were first served tomato bisque with whipped cream on top, followed by turkey with mashed potatoes and sweet potatoes, squash, stewed onions and celery, cranberry sherbet, fruit salad, then caramel ice cream with nuts and cherries in it, then mince pie, then nuts and raisins. Coffee was served in the sitting room. Today's young women might be turned off by the calories and cholesterol, but Helen, at least, was thin and active and never gained a pound while she ate her way through Wellesley. And she loved to eat! Thursday night at five there was a light buffet after which they stuffed, put on their kimonos and read to each other until bedtime. Friday afternoon and Saturday morning there were classes as usual in spite of the small number of participants, and the weekend saw the return of other students.

Helen wrote to her parents that her German instructor had advised her not to plan on taking a second year of German. She was not doing well in that subject. Even so, they were stunned when Helen flunked German that first semester. It was the first and only time Helen ever flunked a course. She hastened to assure her parents that it was not as bad as it sounded. At Wellesley there were only two categories: passed and failed. Since A,B and C were passing with credit, and D was passing, it didn't matter much what you got except for the humiliation of it and the fact that it didn't add as many points when it came to qualifying for offices and societies. She felt certain she could make the grade by June.

It was well known that Wellesley's Freshman year was particularly difficult. A great deal of pressure was put on the students. More left during the year because of stress than failing. Two years later Wellesley eased the program for the Freshman year and Helen's sister, Jane, benefited. Helen might have trouble with German but she had A's in her math subjects and literature. She was proud of her accomplishments in both literature and composition.

Besides the pressure of upcoming exams, Helen had an additional concern -- her source theme. A source theme, as she explained to her family, was really three themes in one; a main theme, then a limited subject under the main one, and a third subject allied to the second. They were the "bugbear of Freshman life." Those three themes were each twenty pages long and "the worst of it is you can't write a thing out of your head, but have to get it all from some authority," thus the name. That was indeed a frustrating situation for the imaginative Helen.

Helen chose for her main theme "The Women of the French Revolution." Her sub-theme dealt with "A Defense of Marie Antoinette" and her third, or allied theme, "The Childhood of Marie Antoinette." "It has been awfully interesting, looking up material for them, but it sure does take the time,"[2] she complained. This experience would prove most valuable when, some years later, she studied at Oxford University and wrote her thesis on Eighteenth Century Female Writers.

While Helen was coping with the stress and strain of academics, the end of 1914 saw the start of the war in Europe. Helen wrote, "We hear nothing but 'war, war, war.' The whole college is doing and giving what they can for Belgian relief." Guest speakers described the horrors of the war to the women, telling them of torture and terrible suffering. By 1915 the talk of war in Europe expanded to talk of the United States becoming involved. Helen wrote to her father, "What do you and the people in Ohio think about our getting into war? I can't believe it will ever come to that."

Not all the speakers talked of war, however. The English poet, John Masefield, later poet laureate, came to read his poetry. Helen described him as long, slim and weary looking. In the middle of his reading, a figure clad in a terra cotta dress waddled down the aisle and settled in the front row. Helen was aghast when she found out it was Amy Lowell. Masefield was followed by Vachel Lindsey. "Believe me, he's a nut," Helen reported.

The ivied halls of Wellesley represented, with the rest of the Seven Sisters and the Ivy League, the finest in academic excellence, social contacts and gracious living. They were places where families sent their offspring to learn to think, to grow and to develop their scope of knowledge. For the most part, the students knew what was expected of them; they could enjoy themselves but their primary responsibility was to learn. Finding a job came later when they knew something.

But times were changing and, with the onset of war, those safe colleges were changing -- never to be quite the same again. In the meantime, in that age of innocence, the end of the academic year brought new college experiences into the lives of the young women at

Wellesley: the traditional hoop race, proms and step singing, to name a few. There was a class play to be written and performed and Helen was on the committee. There were exciting days of anticipation: who would be class president next year; who would hold offices; and who would be invited to join which societies? Wellesley had societies instead of sororities, and they were very important to Helen. She was invited to join (to her) the best -- Alpha Kappa Chi.

Early in her Sophomore year Helen was invited to join Scribblers, a prestigious group of student writers. She was involved and satisfied that her college career was doing nicely. There were many college traditions to participate in and many school songs, both old and new, to learn. Every letter home to the folks related some new experience as well as the sense of excitement and anticipation that permeated the campus. Some have called Helen a wordsmith -- one of those rare people who are able to see not only the details of the panorama around them but to relate the whole picture to others in their writing. Just as she wrote of her college experiences to the family at home, Ohio, Xenia and her family were the subjects of many of her themes and papers. Fellow students and teachers often felt as though they knew those people and places.

Through the years at Wellesley there were subtle signs of change in Helen. The effervescent young girl was growing into a more mature, thoughtful person. She still wrote home regularly and often, but her letters began to sound more like a commitment than the spontaneous outpourings of the early years. Her horizons had broadened but she never lost sight of who she was or what was expected of her. The world had changed drastically. Rather than change drastically herself, she seemed to draw her value system around her like a protective cover.

Chapter 4

❧

Wellesley...the War Years

"All we talk about," wrote Helen to her family in Xenia, "is War, War, War."[1] One weekend in April she went with Wellesley friends to Nahant on the shore, staying in Senator Lodge's cottage while she was there. "We sat on the rocks and watched five torpedo destroyers and a submarine go in and out of the harbor." She told of the flag draped buildings in Boston and recruits marching across Boston Common. Wellesley, in preparation for their role in the war, had instituted a Red Cross nursing course for the young women. Only fifty were able to enroll and Helen was one of the first. New England women were also being instructed in "managing autos" so they could enlist in the Red Cross as ambulance drivers.

Some were leaving school to marry men already enlisted in the military. Others, including one of Helen's best friends, were leaving to go to Europe to help in some capacity. Helen herself thought of leaving school and applied for acceptance as a Yeoman in the Navy to serve at the port in Boston or New York. She wrote home asking for advice about her decision, but she eventually decided it was wiser to graduate first.

In her letters home Helen still mentioned particularly interesting dinners or trips to visit friends or a newly purchased dress, but her letters were noticeably more focused on politics, the war, career possibilities and philisophical concerns.   Even the envelopes for her letters reflected the changing times. Each now bore a red imprint by the post office which read: "Do your bit! BUY A LIBERTY LOAN BOND. Inquire at any bank or post office." In addition the postal rate had skyrocketed from the accustomed two cents to three cents.

When Helen first arrived at Wellesley in 1914, she was eager to share every experience with her family. To some it might seem she wrote home frequently (at least six letters a month for four years) but often she begged her family to understand why she did not write more often. "You say I don't write often but I don't know why you say that." On November tenth in 1917 she finally wrote, "I'm writing this because I said I would -- not because I have time."

In addition to her studies, Helen was involved in many activities one of which was the Equal Suffrage League. She was elected Secretary-Treasurer and was appointed moderator for a series of debates. "I know as much about debating as a rabbit," she complained. Rabbit or no, the debates went off without a hitch and Helen continued to work for Women's Suffrage. She felt her efforts had paid off when Women's Suffrage became the 19th amendment in 1919. Helen was proud that Ohio was the fifth state to ratify it.

Ohio was known to be a Republican state and Greene County and Xenia were staunchly Republican. It followed, then, that when Woodrow Wilson sought re-election in 1916 and ran against Republican Charles Evans Hughs, Helen was avidly interested in the political campaign. Hughes had been Governor of New York State from 1907 to 1910; he served as Associate Justice on the Supreme Court from 1910 to 1916 when he accepted the Republican nomination. Helen and other Santmyers felt he was vastly better qualified to serve as president than "Sister" Wilson, who had been president of Princeton University before becoming President of the United States in 1912. Like another

Democratic president twenty-five years later, he promised to keep America out of war. That won him the election but almost immediately the U.S. was plunged into war. Letters expressing disappointment and concern for the outcome of that election flew back and forth between Xenia and Wellesley. Helen's Father had just been elected to the Xenia School Board, and his daughter wrote to congratulate him. She also told him of an article she had read in the *Boston Herald* on January 29, 1918, that reported Newton D. Baker "was said to have made an impression with his report to Congress on military affairs." Newton Baker had been Mayor of Cincinnati and was not unknown to Mr. Santmyer before Baker left for Washington to become Secretary of War in 1916. As Secretary of War (now referred to as Secretary of Defense) Mr. Baker was responsible for the organizing and provisioning of the army -- two million men.

Helen also brought to Mr. Santmyer's attention an article in the *Saturday Evening Transcript* that was not complimenary to "Sister" Wilson and his friends. It seems that Lloyd George, then Prime Minister of England, and others had demanded an important place for American General Leonard Wood. General Wood was a hero who had commanded the Rough Riders during the Spanish-American War and later became Governor-General of the Philippines. Helen wrote, "You would think he [Wilson] would be ashamed of having stuck him [Wood] off in Kansas someplace." She wanted to know what her father had to say about that!

Helen, at the same time, was concerned about the problem of pro-German sympathizers and pacifists in the United States, especially on the faculty of Wellesley College. Xenia, located in the southwest corner of Ohio, was home to many people of German descent like the Santmyers, but in spite of her German heritage Helen was fiercely patriotic. Consequently, she created and circulated a petition asking for the resignation of those faculty members who were not supportive of the United States. In part it read, "We feel the only justification of a woman's college in war time, is the training which it may offer for more intelligent patriotic service..." Faculty members did not resign from Wellesley College, but they were quieted somewhat by the show of disapproval among the students.

In spite of the war and politics, college life continued. Wellesley women had been held in quarantine because of a measle epidemic. In those days, when people had a contagious disease, they were separated from the public to hold down the spread of the disease. When the quarantine was lifted, however, Helen and her friends sought their favorite twenty-five cent seats at the Copely Theater in Boston and saw a play called *Inside the Lines*. "It was a very exciting play of spies and soldiers at Gibraltar at the out-break of the war." Helen reported that, "It was as clever and amusing as it was exciting."

To add to the enjoyment, the play concerned a family by the name of Sherman from Illinois. Helen's friend Monty [Ellen Montgomery from Hubbards Wood, Illinois] got so excited, "she could hardly be held in her seat when Chicago was mentioned," Helen laughingly remembered. "The father of the stage family," she explained, "was trying to persuade the innkeeper, who was a German spy, to keep them until he could get some money from home. Mr. Sherman, the father, clasped his head and cried, 'Oh, if only you were a brother Elk!'" The reference to the benevolent fraternity got a big laugh from the audience. "He told the hotel keeper he was from Kewanee, Illinois. 'Haven't you heard of Kewanee?' 'No.' 'Haven't you heard of Illinois?' 'No.' 'What! The state Chicago is in?' 'No.' 'Humph! You talk like a New Yorker!' " To those from the Midwest, that scene made the play!

In addition to the play in January, The Chicago Opera Company arrived in Boston in February to present Australian born Nellie Melba in *Faust*, and Galli Curci in *La Traviata*. Unfortunately, an epidemic -- this time it was poliomyelitis -- broke out in the Boston area and once again they were held in quarantine. There was no Salk vaccine with which to immunize them and polio was a devastating disease.

Further trips to Boston were curtailed for the duration of the quarantine. During the last couple of years at Wellesley, Helen visited many friends during the weekends and holidays. It was as if she wanted to squeeze every experience out of those college years. She visited Rebecca [Speck] Vincent's family in Ridgewood, New Jersey, where several other Wellesley friends also lived. There were parties and bridge games and teas and Helen had a wonderful time. She wrote to her family while she was visiting, as usual, and told them everything she knew they wanted to hear. It was a beautiful town with rolling front lawns and large houses. The Vincents were nice people who lived well. They were "the same kind of people as we are... not wealthy or pretentious, just all-round nice." She explained that Mr. Vincent commuted from Ridgewood to his office in New York City every day, leaving early and returning late. She assured her father that he would not enjoy it at all.

While visiting the Vincents they had an outing to Staten Island, taking the same boat there and back. "We could easily imagine we were just back from Europe -- we greeted Liberty as though we hadn't seen her for ages." The girl who played the experienced traveler game on the trains when she was a child was not far from the adult Helen. They thrilled at the sight of the New York skyline and, while in the city, they went to the luxurious Waldorf Astoria Hotel for dinner. "I never felt quite so swell in all my life," Helen exclaimed.

During the Christmas holiday of 1917 Helen visited the Lombards in Cooperstown, New York. Hilda and her brother Hugh, with a small staff of servants, lived in a little white cottage on Lake Street which had a view of Lake Otsego. Cooperstown is the historic town made famous by James Fenimore Cooper in his *Leatherstocking Tales*. It was, and still is, very beautiful countryside. Cooper's Glimmerglass (Lake Otsego) is surrounded by the foothills of the Adirondacks and the tiny village of Cooperstown is nestled at the foot of the lake. In 1917 there were no crowds of tourists and no Baseball Hall of Fame which Helen, always a devoted baseball fan, would have loved. Rather, it was peopled in summer by wealthy families from New York City who had built very large summer houses on the lake shore. In winter it reverted to a sleepy farming village. It was cold -- sometimes dropping to 20° below zero -- and there was always a lot of snow. The sidewalks were plowed by a single horse with tinkling bells pulling a V-shaped sled, sometimes forming snowbanks six feet high.

Like Wellesley, Cooperstown had about three blocks of commercial enterprises. The rest was residential. A grand railroad hotel, The Otesaga, designed in the manner of The Greenbrier and The Homestead in West Virginia, bustled in the summer with golfers, sailors and other guests, but in the winter the hotel was dark and empty. The village that Helen visited was a quiet, sleepy place indeed. But it was beautiful, with wide streets and venerable trees and immaculate houses which represented our country's early history. It was from such a little house on Lake Street that Helen wrote home about her harrowing trip and the Lombards' charming old white house with wrought iron door knobs and hinges...cold but cozy.

Helen wrote that she had taken the pullman train from Boston to Albany, switched to another railroad line's coach car for the trip to Colliers, New York, where she was glad to be met by her friend Hilda for the last leg of the trip. Taking all of the bags and packages, they left the train. They waited till it was almost dark for the little rail car the locals referred to as the "Toonerville Trolley." They climbed aboard taking all the baggage. Underway, the little car lunged from one side to the other as it rolled down the track, coming perilously close to the telephone poles which looked like toothpicks in the high snowbanks. When they finally reached Cooperstown it was dark and cold. They were met by Hugh for the trek to the house on Lake Street and Helen began to relax. The welcoming sight of the blazing fireplace and the cups of hot tea did more than warm Helen's spirit that night. Eventually Hilda and Hugh would move back to their more permanent home in nearby Amsterdam, New York, and Helen would visit them there, never to return to the land of J. F. Cooper.

There were other visits to other friends in New York City, Brunswick, Maine, and the horse country near Bernardsville, New Jersey, where life was quite formal and luxurious. The family dressed for dinner every night, and Helen was pampered by a staff of servants, including a liveried chauffeur. "I never felt so grand in my life," Helen sighed. Education at Wellesley reached far beyond the ivied halls.

In 1917 the best-read book in Helen's circle of friends was the *Book of Princeton Verse*, edited by Alfred Noyes, and published by Princeton University Press in 1916. The book contained poetry by Princeton's class of 1916 and was, the Wellesley women believed, far superior to anything they had produced. Why? They discussed this question endlessly. "Surely our brains are not inferior,"[2] Helen insisted. At a Scribblers meeting it was discussed with Helen's mentor, Miss Shackford, who suggested that perhaps the men wrote better poetry because that was what they set their minds to and they did nothing else. Seldom did one read a poet who was also president of the class and a player on a varsity team! Actually, Miss Shackford knew not of what she spoke, but she impressed those young women and several of them, including Helen, resigned from committees and clubs and offices to concentrate their efforts on their poetry. They would prove themselves!

Spurred on by her sacrifice, Helen wrote a five page article for the Wellesley College Magazine of May 1917. In it she stated, "Princeton has published a whole volume of verse infinitely better than any we have done. We refuse to admit that women are less strong than men; we refuse to admit that our interests are neither so wide nor so deep as theirs... We believe our imaginations are as vivid as theirs, our minds are as keen, but certainly our verse measures far below theirs in all these ways."

Helen continued to explain that the Princeton book, seventy-five poems, dealt with almost every conceivable subject -- as adequately as can be expected of youth. Scribbler productions, on the other hand dealt with child life, nature, historical subjects and -- "timorously" -- with love. Helen noticed that it was not a problem of having fewer things to write about but they were less daring in writing about them. "...few girls brave the hoots of derision that greeted one young poetess who began to read: I was a gargoyle once..."

Helen bemoaned the fact that Wellesley women do not dedicate themselves to their poetry. They have too many social activities, she complained, too much gossip, too many committees and teams. She seemed to have believed that men are not prone to these distractions.

"The trouble is not one of us is going to acknowledge in her heart that she purposes to spend her life writing poetry. The Princeton man is fitting himself for some life profession or business and no circumstance is going to change that profession, whether he has chosen poetry or chemistry." Again, Helen is a bit naive and supposes too much. "The Wellesley girl is serving two masters: she is preparing herself to lead a life of single blessedness if the gods decree, and at the same time is planning to be married." She continued, scathingly, "I speak with utter scorn for myself and friends, but it is true. We are ardent suffragists in theory, yet few believe that career and baby carriages can be managed by the same hand." Many young women today echo her doubts.

Since she was a young child Helen Santmyer had believed that she would never marry. She felt sad for her mother, whom she thought had given up a promising career as an artist for a husband and children. This in spite of the fact that there is no record of a single complaint by her mother, who pursued her art as a hobby in her own studio, supported and encouraged by her husband. But Helen was convinced she would never be a martyr like her mother. It wasn't that she didn't like men. She did. But she would never sacrifice her work for another. This point is re-enforced in *Herbs and Apples* when Derrick, Helen's alter-ego, says, "...married! A girl might as well be dead as married! I refuse to admit that men have better minds than women, but they certainly aren't victims of marriage as women are."[3]

In the end, women of Wellesley were encouraged by Helen to dare to write verse equal to that of Princeton men, whether they were to write for a month or all of their lives. It was a theme that would pervade Helen's books and follow her through her life.

Action-packed days preceding graduation, however, once again distracted them from their verses. There were Wellesley traditions to be observed: the Maypole dance, the hoop race to determine who would be first to marry, the baby carriage race to see who would have the first baby. There were outfits to be assembled. Each event required specific dress. In addition there were plans to be made for the arrival of families. Rooms had to be secured, parties had to be planned, activities organized to entertain the parents and prove they had not wasted their money on a Wellesley education for their daughters -- as Helen's own grandfather believed.

The days hurried by. Then it was all over! In addition to learning, the years at Wellesley had been made up of fun, excitement, joy, dreams and hope -- with just a dash of disappointment and sadness. It was an elixir brewed for youth, never to be tasted again. There were teary good-byes and promises to keep in touch, no matter how unlikely. Helen, already having planned to return to Boston and her closest friends after summer break in Xenia, had no qualms about losing touch.

But Helen was not quite finished with her education. In April, before graduation, Helen wrote to her father about her plans for the future. "It's awfully hard to be as definite as you think I ought to be about what I want to do next year. I want a job with some publishing company in New York, but unless you have pull it's hard to get one without training in typewriting and shorthand. If you are given a position where they are not needed, it is much preferred that you have them anyway." Therefore, the immediate future was already planned and Father, as usual, agreed to finance the project.

Part II

(1919-1924)

"...To Attain
Desirable Ends"

Chapter 5

❧

National Woman's Party in Boston

Upon graduating from Wellesley College Helen returned to Xenia for a summer respite. She would have preferred to be a woman of independent means so she could write unencumbered by other duties such as earning a living. Just as at Wellesley, she wished she could do nothing but write poetry. She wished she were free to do nothing but pursue her writing. The world, however, does not work that way and Helen knew she had to get a job. As her father had said in a letter to her while she was in college, if one wanted to write, it was wise to have some kind of work which would finance such endeavors. To attain desirable ends, one must have desirable employment.

Helen had always assumed there were two paths for her to follow. Preferably, she wanted a job with a publishing company in New York City, the center of the American literary scene. The other career possibility open to her was teaching. World War I had not ended and war service became a third path to consider. There was still talk of the Navy and the Red Cross, and the women even considered going to Armenia to help save the starving people.

Once home in Xenia with her family, however, the summer of 1918 was spent as previous summers had been, and the high dreams of college days were shelved until fall. Wellesley friends, as promised, visited Helen at 111 3rd Street and enjoyed the hospitality of the Santmyers in the big white house -- just as Helen had described it. The summer passed pleasantly and swiftly, but then reality began to raise its ugly head. In the fall of 1918, with renewed vigor, she enrolled in the final phase of her educational preparation -- a quick course in typewriting and stenography. Now armed with the credentials and skills that were expected of every woman, Helen knew she was ready to enter the working arena.

In March 1919, the war was over and so were the plans to go to France or Armenia. It seems they were not needed. So they decided on Boston as a place to begin their careers. It would be like Wellesley only with more freedom. Helen contacted Atlantic Press and Little Brown, but, neither of them had an opening for an entry-level job in the publishing field.

Through her association with the Equal Suffrage League at Wellesley, Helen had contacts which led to a summer job with a similar group in Boston. She finally wrote home to tell her family she had settled on an office job with...the National Woman's Party! Yes, it was the same group of "wild girls who burned President Wilson etc."[1] Helen hastened to assure the Santmyers that she was not required to burn anything or march in the streets. She was hired to manage the phones in the office, take dictation and type the letters from 9 to 5 Monday through Friday and Saturday 9 to 12 noon. Her family were asked to realize that it wasn't a bad job and it was, after all, only temporary.

The office was in a corner building on Park Street and Beacon. It was across from Boston Common and catty-cornered from the State House -- a very convenient location. To make life even more agreeable, Eli and Tim and Monty, her friends from Wellesley, were also on the scene. Eli, was employed at Gardenside Bookstore nearby. "Eli will forever be in the book business -- not much money but books at a discount makes it all worth while."

On March 24 Helen wrote home "to let you know I have worked for a day and am still living. It wasn't much working today -- we cleaned up the office and did nothing else." Helen reported that Mrs. Morey, "charming in spite of her willingness to go to jail," wasn't in the office much. Within a few weeks, Helen was pleased to announce she had been made "headman," or Office Manager. They left her pretty much on her own. She reported to Mrs. Fuller, a pleasant woman from an old family, whom Helen described as having, "bobbed hair, Bostonian shoes, is married with five children but wears no wedding ring."[3]

Since no furnished apartments were available, some of the women took rooms at the Students' Union on nearby St. Steven Street, an easy walk to their places of employment. Helen was not a student, but one of her friends wangled permission for her to become a member.

No suitable apartment was available yet, however, they had been assured something would open up during the summer when residents left the hot city. In the meantime Monty had left for Chicago in spite of protests from the others, but Hilda had finally succumbed to their pleas and agreed to join them for the summer, bringing her Packard, making Wellesley and shore points accessible throughout the summer.

Asked about her finances, Helen wrote to her father that she was managing well. The room at the Students' Union was eight dollars and fifty cents. "They make the beds, supply the sheets and towels and there's only one other person uses the bath." It was a good arrangement. They were quite comfortable but still looking for an apartment which they could all four share. Life couldn't have been much better for young Helen, it seemed.

But guilt must have nagged at her for later in March she wrote to her parents, " Why don't you write to me? If you don't like my job, say so, and I'll get another -- although I've tried all the publishing companies. I feel as though I had been disinherited or something." Hilda, it seems, was trying to talk Helen into joining her in Amsterdam, New York, getting a job there and living in her family's big house. "I suppose I should do as much writing with Hilda egging me on. I wish you would write and advise me."

Finally, an apartment became available, and Helen wrote that after the first of May their new address would be 238 Hemmenway Street. The apartment needed a good deal of work to make it livable for them so the first week of April was spent scrubbing the place down and moving their belongings, which they had begged and borrowed, into the new quarters. It had been a choice between two apartments, neither ideal, but in the end they chose a large airy apartment filled with the landlady's "atrocities." These atrocities included a grandfather clock, marble topped tables and a sideboard "carved to suit the 1870 eye." Today they would all be considered valuable antiques, but to the eyes of those young woman of the Art Deco age, they were atrocities indeed. Once they had each hung their own pictures, placed their own books, covered the undesirable furnishings with fashionable Spanish shawls and applied other stylish touches, they felt quite at home.

Helen, as usual, drew a sketch of the apartment so that her family would know what she was referring to in her letters. The quarters consisted of a large kitchen, bath, two bedrooms, a large entrance hall and a living room which served as Helen's bedroom. Helen described the placement of all the furniture. "My letters must sound like a Ladies Home Journal article." The women felt very fortunate with their new digs. The landlady had originally asked fifty dollars a month for the place, but when she heard they were from Wellesley, she fell on their necks and let them have it for forty dollars -- ten dollars apiece.

The apartment was behind the Christian Science Church and down a little so it was about a forty-five minute walk to the office across from the State House. Helen described her daily walk "down Huntington Avenue to the Boston Public Library, down Boylston to Park Square -- where Tim and Eli drop off, then cut across the Common to the Park Street Church and up Park Street to Beacon.

"At noon Eli walks down Boylston and I walk down Tremont, we meet in front of the Touraine [Hotel] and cut off to Childs for luncheon." Helen bragged that she had learned to eat on one dollar a day, as her friends did. They stopped at the corner drug store for a fifteen cent breakfast which consisted of coffee and four warm crisp buttered pieces of toast. They had their lunch at Childs: chicken hash, spaghetti or baked beans, plus coffee and doughnuts for forty cents. Dinner was usually eaten at the Student's Club around the corner from them: soup, meat "of some indeterminate variety," mashed potatoes and gravy, squash, salad and ice cream...all for forty-five cents. Total: one dollar!

It wasn't all work and no play. To celebrate their new jobs, they decided to go to "Durgan and Parks" for dinner. Durgan Park is a venerable eatery down in the market area where meals are served family-style to college students, business men and tourists. Sawdust on the floor, crusty old waitresses and almost always someone of interest at your table. The place had the charm of an old butcher shop but its reputation was founded on wonderful food at reasonable prices.

Helen and her friends gave up the idea of ordering Durgan Parks' famous slabs of beef and settled for boiled lobster with all the trimmings, plus strawberry shortcake or pie and ice cream. "We had an uproarious time," Helen reported to her parents, "and the meals cost us each eighty-five cents." After dinner, they all walked up to Trinity Place Station and took the nine o'clock train to Wellesley to spend the weekend at AKX, see Helen's sister Jane and the other underclassmen that they still knew.

Monday morning saw them back working at their various occupations. The problem with Helen's job was that it was boring. She really had little to do and none of it was the least bit challenging. "I opened the mail," she complained, "sent out some notices...sat some more until the treasurer came in...she went over the books with me and I must say right now, I know more about bookkeeping accounts than she does so you can imagine!" But other things compensated for the job. Life was quite pleasant. It was not a career, after all, and she was able to support herself for the most part.

For a young woman with great promise, eager to take on the literary world, Helen was frustrated by the humdrum job she found herself engaged in. Who of us has not had some entry level job in which we felt underutilized? In the midst of her frustration, her friend Hilda finally arrived in Boston with her Packard car. Helen said she believed Hilda's main purpose in coming was to try again to persuade Helen to return with her to Amsterdam, New York. "I can't bear to think of her alone in that house [Hilda's brother, Hugh, had taken off to seek his own fortune] and she won't come to Boston or New York until fall for several reasons...

"I have sent some verse to some magazines and though I expect nothing to come of it, I feel as though I had got started in the right direction. Do you think it would be terrible to leave Boston, after wishing for so long to be here? I wish you would write and advise me."

In the end, Helen stayed in Boston with her friends through the summer as planned, and Hilda changed her mind and stayed with them. When the summer was over and the job commitment fulfilled, they headed for New York City, where they believed the real excitement was.

Chapter 6

❦

Scribners and Sons
In New York City

In September 1919, when Helen boarded the train at South Station in Boston, she knew it was the closing of a chapter in her life. A new chapter was about to begin. In New York she changed trains in Pennsylvania Station and boarded the familiar Train Twenty One which had taken her and her family back and forth to Ohio so many times. Noah, the porter she had known all her life, looked smart in his starched white coat as he helped her with her luggage. He inquired about her family, asked how her summer had been and what her plans were for the future.

Helen told him about her summer job in Boston and her plans for starting her career in New York City after a brief visit with her family in Xenia. He would be seeing her in a few weeks for her return trip.

It was a beautiful October day when Helen arrived in New York, and her Wellesley friend, Hefty, met her at Penn Station. It was so nice to be met by someone. They did not go directly to Helen's apartment. Hilda, with whom she would be sharing the place, wouldn't be in until later that night so she and Hefty went downtown to the apartment Hefty shared in Greenwich Village. Helen was impressed with the living arrangements her friends had made, and she thought they had exaggerated the inconveniences when they described the place to her. The two young women had dinner and a nice visit before Helen headed uptown to her new home at 122 East 82nd Street. There, she could hardly believe her luck. What greeted her was a spacious light apartment painted green with white woodwork and mahogany doors with stylish glass door knobs. As usual, Helen drew a floor plan to explain the layout to her family who were anxious to know what kind of living arrangements their daughter had. To the left of the entry, next to the kitchen, was a maid's room and bath; straight ahead was the large light living room with a large dining room adjoining it; behind those rooms were two large bedrooms and a bath. It was a far cry from the garret she had expected.

The Santmyers had arranged for Beacher, a black girl from Xenia, to accompany Helen to New York. She was to look after the young working women. Helen assured her family, "Beacher has proved to be a treasure -- perfectly wonderful cook -- does all the buying and planning of meals -- wears a uniform -- and from the correctness and fastidiousness of her service might have worked for the Vanderbilts. Isn't it amazing!"[1] Heaven help the *working girls.*

Friday was Helen's first full day in New York, and she spent it unpacking her trunks and setting about finding a job. She made a list of all the quality publishers, then decided to start her search at the bottom of Fifth Avenue and work her way uptown with the idea that the last place would be the closest to her apartment. As luck would have it, the first office she went to was Scribners and Sons. They offered her a job on the spot. Helen was so pleased she accepted on the spot. She wrote home to tell her family. "I'll start by saying that I have a job -- also saying that Father will probably have a fit because they won't start me on more than fifteen a week. But it's exactly the sort of job I wanted so I didn't have the heart to turn it down."[2]

The job was in the book part of Scribners, not the magazine part for which Helen had hoped. Her duties were partly stenographic and partly taking care of the proofs, seeing that authors and editors got the proofs on the appointed days and taking care of the original drawings, seeing that they were returned to the artists as promised. Scribners promised a raise in three or four weeks, if Helen proved herself.

With Hefty and Vedder in an apartment downtown and Speck and Jo working nearby, Helen felt secure among her old college group. It was true, however, that one-by-one they were marrying and dropping by the wayside. So were her friends in Xenia. Every time she read an announcement or received an invitation it caused a twinge of regret. No wedding caused her more mixed emotions than that of an old friend from Xenia who married a male friend of Helen's who had escorted Helen to many dances, hayrides, picnics and parties. He had expressed interest in Helen and had even kissed her, but Helen, true to her childhood promise, told him that marriage was out of the question for her but they would always remain friends. When she heard he had married another she was torn between being happy for him and acknowledging that a door was forever closed to her. However, Helen was still a young woman with the world in front of her, after all, and most of her close friends were still unmarried, trying to make their marks in the world.

Kate, a Xenia woman who had gone to Europe after Wellesley, wrote to Vedder often and told her she was still in Christiania with no immediate hope of getting to Russia. Christiania had been known as Oslo, capital of Norway, until 1624 when it was destroyed, rebuilt, and renamed for Kristian -- King of Norway. It was known as Christiania until 1925, when it reverted to Oslo. Kate, it seemed, had been in trouble with the YWCA on a question of her "heresy." It all was resolved but Kate threatened to resign and join the Free Working People of Norway. No one was surprised. "Same old Kate," Helen commented.

Two of Helen's friends were writing movies for that new industry. Vedder, working to place orphans, was about to leave on one of her many trips with an orphan in tow. She had been arrested earlier in Chicago as a kidnaper, "securing her release only upon showing her credentials." Hefty was out of work, having left the hospital, and she couldn't find another job. "I don't think she has looked very hard as I had no trouble,"[3] Helen confided with little sympathy.

Hilda, who had no need to work but was employed at the library, as usual, went shopping -- sometimes taking Helen with her. On one such shopping spree Hilda ordered "a stunning dress from Stein and Blaines -- a sporty place where you sit on a divan and models prance up and down before you showing off things."[4] On the way home from that shopping trip Helen saw the king and queen of England twice. Once they passed by in automobiles going up Fifth Avenue, then just as Helen reached the mansion, they "went into the Vanderbilts" to some sort of reception. "They are much more foreign and French-looking than their pictures, and they looked awfully loud, particularly the king." By August 1920, Helen informed her family that at Scribners she now had an assistant, "as everyone insists on calling Bernice. Now, I'm going to have more leisure to write letters!" Her boss, Mr. Bridges, had spent the weekend with Mrs. Corinne Roosevelt Robinson and together they had planned a book about Teddy Roosevelt. Now Mr. Bridges was dictating the outline of the book to Helen. Helen liked T.R. and the book was interesting, but she would have preferred working on her own book.

By the end of August 1920, Helen was planning her vacation. It was scheduled for September 10th through September 25th, but Helen was hoping to put it off for a week. Hilda and a friend were planning to drive to Chicago and wanted Helen to join them. Helen was hoping to do that before going home to Xenia. Hilda's friend was a tennis champion from a district in Minnesota, and was in New York to play in a tournament at Southhampton which Helen and Hilda went to see. Helen liked the friend and the trip to Chicago seemed like fun.

They were now working women, but much of the young student days lingered. When the group got together to read John Masefield's new book of poetry, they all remembered when he had appeared at Wellesley to read his work. Scribners had just published the new volume. Helen had worked with him during the process so there was a personal interest this time. When the reading was over, Helen and Vedder went out to get a watermelon and ginger ale and grape juice, which became their dinner. There were no carry-out places down the street in those days. They all enjoyed an old-fashioned spread like they had in their college days.

When Helen returned from her vacation she found there wasn't a great deal of work at the office. However, Galsworthy was coming over soon. But "there is no prospect of anything thrilling." She was becoming quite blasé about her work. She occasionally worked with Ernest Hemingway and F. Scott Fitzgerald, but she found that less than thrilling, too. She did not like the coarse, macho, loud Hemingway at all, and she found Fitzgerald to be a spoiled young man and often drunk. A career in the literary world was certainly not filled with excitement. But it was a living, and sometimes her boss would give her an additional assignment -- like indexing a book over the weekend -- which would put an extra twenty dollars in her paycheck.

On October 31st, Helen wrote to tell her family she had sent off her ballot and hoped it got there in time. Helen, always interested in politics, had followed the campaign and, though she felt that a Republican victory was assured, casting her ballot was important. Warren G. Harding, a Republican from Ohio, was indeed elected, but he died suddenly in 1923 and was replaced by Calvin Coolidge.

Wellesley was never far from Helen's thoughts and she decided to return for initiations at AKX. "You no doubt think it was a wild thing to do," she wrote to her parents, "but I decided it would be my last bat [a "bat" was the term of the day for a "fling" or a short holiday] before starting to save money to go to England on -- and I had just enough money, since Father paid my way back." Helen's intentions to save money were sincere, but there was always a dress or a bat or a dinner or some reason that called for more money. Her father always seemed ready to accommodate her.

As an excuse for returning to Wellesley, Helen used the fact that she needed to talk to her former mentor, Miss Shackford, about going back to Wellesley to teach. The dull everyday business of the publishing world, especially at the bottom of the ladder, was beginning to wear down her resolve. She did some writing, but she thought nothing serious could be done while she worked full-time. Returning to Wellesley seemed like the perfect answer. Unfortunately, she didn't plan very well. Miss Shackford was gone for the weekend when Helen arrived. Helen didn't get to talk with Miss Shackford but she did get to talk with her old friend K. B. -- "and she is crazy about teaching there," Helen reported. She also talked to K. B. about the need for getting a graduate degree in order to teach. Helen thought of the University of Cincinnati where her parents had gone. K. B. said she was sure that a Masters of Arts from there would be as good as Radcliff. Helen immediately wrote to the registrar at UC and asked for catalogues.

The weather was glorious that weekend and Helen had a wonderful time at Wellesley. She always did. But she had to admit they had strange people in Scribblers now, and she couldn't say much good about the new AKX people either (although she confessed she had little to judge them on). She felt strange because she knew so few people at Wellesley now but K.B. was there to go back to, after all. The initiations brought many old alums for a mini-reunion but in general there were not many familiar faces any more.

When Helen returned from her weekend in Wellesley, she found another old college friend, Tim, had written to say she missed seeing Helen when she was home because she was busy getting engaged. "It's a pretty good excuse," Helen admitted. The young man was Francis Wright from Columbus -- no money but lots of brains. Helen only hoped he was nice enough for her friend. Helen and Tim remained friends for the rest of their lives. Tim died a year or two after Helen.

In November Helen celebrated her 25th birthday when Hilda, Ad and a few others took her out for dinner to an Italian restaurant on 11th Street in Greenwich Village. On Thanksgiving, Budge, another of the Wellesley gang, and her husband joined the group for a traditional dinner -- turkey with all the trimmings plus a birthday cake with chocolate turkeys for favors. That group joined another group that night, including three husbands. "It was all very gay."

Fashion was still a topic in letters to her mother and, with no clothing allowance from Father since leaving college, Helen would write to her mother enlisting help. On November 30, she asked her mother to consider a picture she enclosed. Couldn't Miss Osterly, the family seamstress in Xenia, make a dress from the picture? Maybe Miss Osterly could only make the top and not the skirt, or the skirt to go with that waist? "I know it is meant for a suit but the skirt could be fastened to a lining and the coat effect could go on over it. And tell her I must have it for the holidays!" Poor Miss Osterly! Sometimes Helen was not very sensitive. She didn't realize what pressure she could put upon others. Her sister Jane probably commented on her thoughtlessness.

The more Helen thought about Christmas, the more she wanted to go home. She began to work on her family. "If you and Father gave me money, would it be enough for one way?" She thought she could probably manage to buy a ticket for one way. As usual, good old Mother and Father came through. They always wanted their children to be able to come home when they could.

While Helen was in Xenia for the holidays she discussed the possibility of leaving the publishing field for the teaching profession, always her alternative career path. Her friends in New York were encouraging her to stay with them, of course. They argued that she hadn't been in New York very long and she hadn't really given it a chance. Besides, they thought she was moving along quite well at Scribners. New York was the center of the publishing world. Why did she want to waste her talents teaching kids? Her argument was that she was not able to pursue her own writing while working for Scribners and teaching would give her that opportunity. She had always considered teaching as an option and Miss Shackford had agreed. Also, there was the problem of her health.

When Helen was a small child she nearly died from the results of undulant fever, a disease caused by tainted milk or meat. It was all too common in the early part of the twentieth century but seldom seen today because of meat and milk inspections. Much like rheumatic fever, it could leave its victims with lasting disabilities. For Helen, it had meant years of not being able to do this or that and being told she must be careful and not get too tired. It also meant being confined to bed with high fevers and painful joints. There was little the doctors of the time could do for patients.

For a child who had had fragile health, Helen had passed four remarkably healthy years at Wellesley College. In two hundred letters, the only mention of her health was in one letter when she said she was recovering from a cold. Similarly, in Boston she had had no recurring symptoms. But now, in New York, she complained that the old problems which had plagued her in her youth were back. The Santmyers, ever concerned about Helen's health, encouraged her to return home. Father would finance the move and she could worry about another job when she was fully recovered.

Scribners thought Helen was doing well in their employ. They had given her a couple of raises, she had been given an assistant and she had been transferred to the magazine part which had been her original preference. Consequently, they were surprised when she notified them that she would be leaving, but she was convinced a return to Wellesley College to teach would enable her to continue her own writing.

On August 13th, 1921 Scribners Magazine, at 5th Avenue and 48th Street, sent Helen a note:

Here both with letters and with art,
You've played a useful, helpful part,
Kept peace that goes with quiet ways,
Won friendly thoughts for all your ways.

JBC

To Miss Helen Santmyer
With Every Good Wish From Her Associates.

The New York experience came to an end. Helen returned to Xenia.

Chapter 7

∞✦∞

Wellesley Revisited

Before Helen left New York City she had written a few magazine articles and some poetry, but she hadn't had much luck getting them published. She had also begun work on *Herbs and Apples*, her first novel. However, working at Scribners, handling correspondence and the manuscripts of others -- left Helen little time to work on her own projects. The idea of teaching at Wellesley appeared to be a solution to her problems. She liked academia, she loved Wellesley and she knew writing and teaching had been a successful combination for many people.

Wellesley was delighted to offer her a job and have Helen back in the fold. Miss Lockwood and the beloved Miss Shackford, now about forty-seven, were still Helen's friends and they would remain her mentors. There were others from the old days, including K.B. (Katharine C. Balderston), a member of Wellesley's class of 1916 and a friend of Helen's from her undergraduate years who would help make life interesting. So with excitement and enthusiasm, tinged with a little resignation because New York had not proved to be successful, Helen arrived on the Wellesley campus to undertake her new duties in the fall of 1922.

As it turned out, she was not to teach but would be an assistant in the Department of English Literature...that meant handling some correspondence, reading students' papers and generally performing the more odious tasks of a college professor. Later, while Helen was a student at Oxford, some friend exclaimed that Oxford was fortunate to have a former member of the Wellesley College faculty with them. She reported in a letter to her family that they little realized what an unimportant person she had been on that faculty.

Helen had not yet arrived at Wellesley when in June 1922, at a meeting of the Department of English Literature, the question arose of who should teach Course 101 in the spring term of the following year. The secretary's notes stated: "The possibility of Miss Santmyer's being permitted to take that [course] was mentioned. No decision was reached."[1] The chairman of the department was "empowered to settle any unimportant matters" that might come up during that last term. Unable to teach and unchallenged by her job, Helen busied herself with her writing. She was continuing work on her first novel, *Herbs and Apples* and getting it ready for submission.

By 1923, the novel was finished and in the hands of Houghton Mifflin, the publisher. With her writing project finished, Helen was more frustrated than ever. She approached Miss Lockwood. They discussed the fact that in order to have teaching responsibilities in a first-rate college like Wellesley one needed to have at least one advanced degree. Miss Lockwood and Miss Shackford, both women of influence in their field, offered to help Helen in any way they could to obtain a scholarship or a grant for further study. Helen first considered Radcliff at nearby Cambridge, Massachusetts and sent for the necessary information and applications. Again Miss Lockwood suggested that it might be less costly and just as prestigious to attend the University of Cincinnati near Helen's home in Ohio. Once more Helen sent for the necessary applications and forms.

Bored with her work-a-day life, Helen felt a little like a second-class citizen at Wellesley. Gone were her glory days when she was a gifted student and participated in all aspects of campus activities. To make things worse, her friend KB, only two years ahead of her, had a Masters Degree and was an instructor, not a lowly assistant. She was glad to have a good friend on campus but somehow things were not as they had been years before. To alleviate some of the stress caused by her new situation, Helen began to research her family history. Geneology sources were easily available, it would be fun, it would fill some of the empty hours and the results would please her mother. She started with *Motley's History of the United Netherlands*[2] in search of Martin Schenck's background. (See the Santmyer genealogy.) She wrote to urge her mother to undertake genealogical research herself, "Then when we know which your ancestors were, I could look up all the gossipy items about them."[3] To illustrate: Helen related the fact that Martin, according to Motley, "never smiled and was never sober." If that didn't interest her mother, how about the fact that "the first Obadiah Holmes was whipped and banished from Salem in the seventeenth century because they didn't like his religion." He went to Newport, it was related, and then to New Jersey where he became one of the original settlers. "...by 1790 his descendants numbered 8000." "That sounds like a fish story," Helen scoffed.

Life at Wellesley still consisted of many parties and teas and dinners and Helen still had opportunities to go into Boston to shop. She didn't make a lot of money, but at least what she spent now was hers, not her father's. Mother continued to help out by sending Helen clothes from time to time. Upon receiving an exceptionally pretty blouse, Helen wrote her thanks and added that she "needed clothes badly."[4]

By the spring of 1924 Helen knew she would not return to Wellesley the coming fall. Wellesley had submitted her name as a candidate for a Rhodes scholarship at Oxford in England and she had been selected. There were academic ties between the two schools as Helen would learn later.

By the end of the academic year all was decided and the arrangements were made for a three year stint at Oxford. At the end of that time Helen would receive a BLD -- Bachelor of Literature Degree, "...devised for American students," Helen would claim later. In the U.S. three years of study would qualify one for a PhD. There was little time to pack and make preparations for the trip, taking the train to Canada and sailing from Montreal. Twenty-nine-year-old Helen was about to embark on one of her greatest experiences.

Part III

(1924-1927)

The Oxford Years

Chapter 8

❧

The Crossing

Many telegrams and letters were exchanged between Helen and her father during June 1924. On June 1, her father wrote to confirm that Helen and her new friend Helen Bower were booked into Room 31, two outside berths on Deck 'B' of the Canadian Pacific steam liner, Montcalm. It was due to sail August 29 from Montreal to Liverpool. In 1924, people did not fly. The travel to Europe was done by ocean liner and it took planning and time.

Originally Mr. Santmyer had written, "The Canadian Pacific Line has a fine reputation for service and attention...Note, you are located on the most desirable deck."[1] But, because of a last-minute date change, Helen would not be on the most desirable deck after all; she would be comfortable, however, and the cost of the accommodations remained the same -- $150.00 for the crossing. Although the berths were not as far forward as he had wanted them to be, he felt they were far enough forward so that Helen would not suffer from seasickness, a common ailment among inexperienced travelers. "Water does not seem to affect any of this family," her father hastened to assure her.

Helen's father had also planned the arrival for her. She was to take a train from Liverpool south through Birmingham and Oxford and

"London," he said, "is just around the corner..."[2] about as far from Oxford as Xenia was from Cincinnati. Mrs. Santmeyer was not wholly in favor of the arrangements. She felt Helen was leaving too early and incurring unnecessary expenses. "I suppose, chiefly," wrote her father, "because she would like to have you stay home as long as possible." Father, on the other hand, felt Helen should take advantage of the time she had and see as much of Europe as she could. "Sorry I can't go along...you'll have to tell us all about it and all about England." He assured her they would follow her travels on the maps.

Mr. Santmyer's last instructions included Helen's expected visit to see her mother's Cousin Caroline Hooven Squires who lived in Chateauroux, not far from Paris, France. Helen might not remember her cousin but Caroline remembered her and wanted to see her very much. The area was beautiful and not hard to reach from Paris. Helen could take the railroad from Paris to Bordeaux, go through Orleans to Chateauroux, "...about as far from Paris as Cincinnati to Columbus [four hours in 1924]."

Helen assured her father that after seeing London museums with Helen Bower, who knew her way around the city, she would go to Paris and subsequently see Cousin Caroline.

"Don't dally with your arrangements now, as time is getting shorter than you realize," Father cautioned in his last letter before her departure. He, as usual, made sure she had enough money. He related the latest family happenings, assured her they were all well and closed by saying, "As for me, I go quietly and meekly about my daily labors."

August 30, 1924 began the first of many letters from Helen, as promised, to keep her family informed about everything, every place and everybody. Detroit and the train ride to Montreal were "hellishly hot," Helen complained. In 1924, no air conditioning made the trip very uncomfortable. The train ride was uneventful and, although her luggage arrived, it was not without damage when they finally reached Montreal. But the two young women were not daunted. They had been invited to have dinner with Bower's friend Rene, a doctor with offices in that

Canadian city. "Rene's apartment is quite luxurious with offices, x-ray rooms and so forth. She has many beautiful things in her apartment." There were four at dinner that night. Rene's friend, Miss Helen Hague, did the carving at the sideboard, Helen reported. "The English in Canada seem to keep their customs. The food was impossible -- out of politeness I passed it over."

The two Helens sailed the following day. "The cabin," she wrote, "is very nice -- clean and blue and white, but it is very tiny and there is no room for flowers in the cabin. The stewardess took them down to the dining table." The stewardess, it seemed, was almost too friendly for the reserved Helen, but she was determined she didn't want to snub the girl so, "we chatter with her when she appears. The ship sailed past Quebec, with the Hotel Frontenac dominating the whole scene -- magnificent!"

Helen, not yet a world traveler, found it interesting that the young couple who had been on the train to Montreal with her, now had steamer chairs next to her on the SS Montcalm (built in the shipyards of Clyde, Scotland). She described her traveling companions as "young, nice looking but, my, very English, which means strangely dressed -- he wears baggy trousers. She is long and bony, tanned, red-cheeked, with short light hair, [wearing] a wide-rimmed black hat, white stockings and black shoes." Helen didn't miss a detail and she firmly believed no one should wear white stockings and black shoes.

As Helen described every meal, tea and spread in her letters home from Wellesley College, so she continued to tell her parents what she knew they wanted to know. "I suppose you are interested -- we had beef broth, macaroni and cheese, coffee and cheese and crackers for dessert." The regimen of the day included breakfast at 8:30, luncheon at 1:00, dinner at 7:00, plus mid morning beef tea and afternoon tea and sandwiches. The food was plain but quite good. The ship was not nearly full, Helen commented, for there were many empty cabins around them, and she thought they should have had more attention from the Canadian Pacific Line. But she had to acknowledge that they were "at a table with decent people," which made the trip more interesting.

It was going to be a fine crossing, Helen believed, because the St. Lawrence was calm, "...if it weren't for the slight vibration you would never know the boat was moving." She closed her first shipboard letter, "With lots of love to you all, and a tremendous amount of gratitude for everything." It was a heartfelt sentiment she would express many times in the next three years.

The ship had been out for two days when it left the St. Lawrence and headed for the open seas, sailing between Newfoundland and Labrador, referred to as "the strait." The captain told the passengers that he almost always took the northern route and followed the coast of Labrador all the way so that they could see the "bleak and dreary coast of the provinces." The weather was glorious and Helen was feeling, "as strong as an ox." The rest and the routine and the fresh air gave her an opportunity to recover from the hectic days before the sailing.

Aware that her parents had never had the experience of traveling by ocean liner, Helen took every opportunity to let them share her experiences -- like the bath. "The baths are most fun of anything," she told them. She had elected to have two baths a day to start -- she wanted to make sure she would be clean even if she couldn't "stagger down the passage" every day. There was a bath stewardess whose job it was to assign bath times and see to it the tub was filled properly. "The tub is filled with salt water -- hot -- and on a board across the tub is a pan of fresh water. You have to scrub with the fresh water because the soap won't lather in the sea water. Then you soak in the salt and , finally rinse with fresh. The result is the vigor of an Amazon!"

Once upon the high seas, Helen succumbed to a little seasickness during a rather bad storm. She tried to take her mind off the storm and not watch, "first an expanse of heaving gray sea and then an expanse of cold gray sky," over and over again. Most of the passengers were worse off than she was, she assured her father, remembering his family pride. "I was homesick and, remembering all the good times we had this summer, didn't see why I had ever thought I wanted to leave home." Finally the storm subsided and the ship returned to a gentle roll.

During the course of the voyage the ship's Chief Engineer gave them a tour of the engine room, one of the highlights of the trip. The Montcalm was an oil-burning ship, a big advantage over the older coal-burning ones. In the first place, he told them, there were no stokers now -- only four men who watched the fires instead of twenty-five as there used to be. Also, there was no longer any overpowering heat and this engine room was "all neat and clean as a pin."

On Friday, the end of the first week at sea, Helen reported heavy fog somewhere between Scotland and the Isle of Man, "so heavy I couldn't see." Finally they reached the north coast of Ireland, not emerald at all, she declared, but only black and gray. By that night they were in the river and would dock in Liverpool on Saturday morning. She had arrived!

Chapter 9

❧

Oxford Arrival

On September 8th Helen was ensconced in London at the Basil Street Hotel, a modest place on Knightsbridge SW3. The hotel was on the west side, just over the line in Belgravia, between Sloane Street and Brompton Road. When she arrived she hurried to get a letter off to her parents who would be waiting to hear of her safe arrival. How fortunate she was, she told her family, to have a double room with a bath, "which is rarer in England than a furnace, even."[1] The bath was beautiful with marble walls and a porcelain tub. All this grandeur was in the most fashionable part of town and was hers for the reasonable sum of 27 shillings [about five dollars].

On that first day she had already seen the wax museum, the British Museum, several palaces and many other sights with her new friend Connie. Connie was a good guide, it seems, for she was very cosmopolitan, had lived a long time in Brussels, Belgium and was "so very French." She was also very fashionable and Helen, always impressed by quality, was surprised to learn that Connie's gorgeous new hat cost only 29 francs -- about $1.50 in US currency!

It was the day of the St. Giles street fair and promised to be an exciting, if noisy, day which started with its setting up at 4:30 in the morning. The streets were already crowded. Aside from the fair, however, that first day in London had been busy indeed. Because she had seen Wellesley's President, Miss Pendleton, at a meeting of University Women in Christiana, Helen had been able to meet the principal of the Society of Oxford Home and get a tour of the residence.

After the tour she went to a bank her father had suggested and opened an account from which she would pay her bills. The banks in Oxford were not equipped to accommodate international money exchanges so it was necessary to make the arrangements for her future banking before she left for the university.

Helen and Connie had tea before visiting the National Gallery -- "it was immense." It wasn't as exciting as she had expected it to be, but the Italian Art, the portraits by Whistler, Gainsborough and the others made a great impression on her. While the National Gallery may have been a disappointment, the British Museum "came up to our highest expectations," especially, she thought, the Greek sculptures and the gold ornaments which her mother would have loved.

"I can't be thankful enough that I'm going to be able to come back." (Helen's vast research for her thesis would be cause to bring her back to London many times.) "Even when we aren't sightseeing but just wandering around, every minute is just fascinating. I only wish you were here," she wrote wistfully. As Helen had thrown herself into life at Wellesley, she was determined to make the most of these years in Europe. Whatever might come, those experiences could never be taken from her.

On Tuesday the two young women took a walking tour. They traveled from Charing Cross to Bedlam to the admiralty, seeing the horseguards on the way. They went to Downing Street and walked up to No.10, but we "did not touch the knocker, which they say is the latest fad." In more modern times, security would make such a liberty impossible. Wednesday they went to Westminster Abbey, Parliament, the Thames, and St. Paul's Cathedral. "A whole history lesson around the Towers and the Crown Jewels," Helen exclaimed with delight. It was like walking into the pages of her history book where everything came to life! She sent her parents a colored map of London so they could follow her travels and she also sent them a map of the Towers with her letter. There was even more on her tour, including The Old Curiosity Shop [of Charles Dickens fame], Fleet Street, Goldsmith's grave, an Elizabethan arch and the Inns of Court, including Inner Temple and Middle Temple.

After two very full days of sightseeing in London, Helen and Connie were ready to depart for Dover and their trip to Paris. They were scheduled to leave Dover at 11:00 am and expected to be in Paris by 6:00 pm, in time for dinner. Helen would go to visit Cousin Caroline the next day.

Only the pleasure of meeting Aunt Florence, Cousin Caroline, and her three children could have softened the disappointment of missing her old Wellesley friend, Hilda, who had been in London with her husband and had hoped to visit with Helen. But the good times with Caroline were worth it. "We have more in common than I have with any of my other relatives," Helen wrote enthusiastically. "I think we have the same tastes in antiques, books, pictures and so forth."

The two walked the roads of Chateauroux, sometimes alone, sometimes with the children. They saw the farmhouses gathered together in small villages -- "filthy but picturesque," Helen noticed. They saw peasants in the fields and vineyards gathering grapes and watching their flocks. They enjoyed picking blackberries along the road and eating them as they walked...nothing so delicious as freshly picked berries.

The tour included seeing the very old house which served as the school for Caroline's children and the ruins of an old tower on the edge of town. Helen thought Caroline a very good sport because she climbed to the top with Helen to see the wonderful view of the village spread out below them. "...if they liked me as much as I liked them, I should be very happy," Helen declared.

With reluctance, Helen said au revoir to her newly found relatives and took the train to Paris and Dover, but as she neared London "the atmosphere grew very murky -- I couldn't tell whether it was fog or smoke -- you could see it creeping over the [landscape], the trees standing up like ghosts." She decided it was really smoke because she could smell and taste it, but it wasn't unpleasant. "London wouldn't be London without it." [It would be many years before London would ban the use of fireplaces and clean up their famous fog.] One day of shopping and sightseeing in London and she was off to Oxford, anxious to be settled at last.

On October 16th Helen wrote to her mother from 8 Norham Road. Because women were not allowed to live at the University, Helen had made arrangements to live in the village at the home of the two Miss Lees during her years at Oxford. The two young women had given a tea in Helen's honor so that she could meet, among others, Miss Adeline Aldrich, who would become her good friend, and Miss Lock, who was to be Helen's sponsor while she was a student. Helen also tried to explain the relationships to her mother. She had gone to see Miss Burrows, the principal, "because it is the thing to do." She explained that every student had a supervisor who looks after the student's welfare. Helen was assigned Miss Ady; under Miss Ady was the tutor.

For new graduate students at St. Anne's College, Oxford there were many rules and regulations to adjust to. "Students over twenty-five years old are exempt from most of them." Those over twenty-five were given keys and could come and go as they pleased, but Helen said she didn't need one. "Ours is hung outside the door, in the provincial way." Most of the rules meant little to Helen, but one she found troublesome: caps and gowns must be worn at all academic appointments and always after 8:30 pm, unless attending a dance or the theater. The worst part of the rule was the fact that the cap and gown, which cost all of 18 shillings for both, were hideous, guaranteed to produce in anyone "the proper spirit of humility." Helen did not wear the cloak of humility very well. "The gowns are short," she complained, "only a little longer than a suit coat, with broad streamers from the shoulders instead of sleeves."

The caps she described as "four-cornered affairs which should be worn so as to be flat across the top of the head," but most women, it seemed, wore them pulled down around their ears like tam o'shanters.

Miss Lock, the sponsor Helen met at the Lees' tea, lived in a house built into the cloister wall adjacent to the cathedral. There she, too, gave a tea for Helen. Helen always tried to paint verbal pictures for her family so that they could follow her experiences as closely as possible. The guests at the tea were not spared Helen's pen. The Canon himself was there, "a dried up little old man" who asked Helen dumb questions about America. "Did the Indians leave books and written records?" Helen described her hostess as "very dignified and very much the lady but decidedly stupid." The Americans commented on the fact that the students at Oxford didn't seem to put much time in on their studies. The English then felt obligated to defend Oxford. They said they "worked sometimes too." Helen told her family she could see no evidence that Oxford students worked much at all. She compared notes with Muriel Morris, a new acquaintance from Wellesley's class of 1922, who, after a year at Oxford, thought they must work while others slept.

Helen was becoming friends with the two Miss Lees, one of whom invited Helen and Adeline Aldrich to the well-known Boar's Hill to see the view. It was worth the three mile walk. From there one could see the spires of Oxford and the place where John Masefield lived. They "leaned on the fence and looked through the slope in the hills, across the college to the blue distance beyond." They picked blackberries, which they ate on the way home, "through the fertile fields and hedgerows and... buttercups in bloom." Helen described the thatched-roof pub they passed as "not quaint for the benefit of tourists," but an everyday pub frequented by blond, rosy Anglo-Saxon locals. Helen would return to Boar's Hill many times and show it to visitors, but the joy of that first experience couldn't be matched.

One of the most impressive places at Oxford for Helen was The Bodleian, and it was there that Helen would spend many hours researching material for her thesis. "The reading room," Helen explained, "is in 'Radcliff Camera', a round building of classical (more or less) design which stands alone in the center of a small square." The original Bodleian Library was destroyed and replaced in the 17th Century through the efforts of the educator, Sir Thomas Bodley. The Bodleian receives a copy of every book published in Great Britain. When using the Bodleian all books must be used in the reading room, which, Helen noted, was no bigger than the reading room in the library at Wellesley College. "It would not seem there is a very large number of zealous students."

The Bodleian would be the site of Helen's daily work, but because it was not wired for electricity the working hours were short. "One can't read after four o'clock in the afternoon and," Helen complained, "it is so dark and gloomy one can hardly see at noon." The oldest part of Duke Humphrey's ancient and beautiful library was built in the 15th Century. It is a "very fine example of Perpendicular Gothic...with a rafted ceiling, beamed in checkerboard, with coats-of-arms painted between the beams." The library was known to be the largest in Europe, next to the British Museum in London and Le Biblioteque Nationale in Paris. The whole experience was like living in her history book.

To Helen, life for women at the University seemed ridiculous. First she was asked to prove she could do research. Having proved to be a successful student at Wellesley, she was insulted. Then there was the matter of her thesis topic. Her original topic had already been done so that meant a search for an appropriate alternative. In the meantime, nothing involving her tutor or sponsor could be resolved until the thesis topic was approved, a loss of valuable time. In addition the "girls" -- at this time Helen was twenty-nine -- were required to wear dark suits, stockings, black shoes, white shirt and black tie all topped by the ridiculous cap and gown. So clad, they lined up in alphabetical order, two-by-two, for the walk down the street to the Divinity School to participate in the Matriculation Ceremony. Once at the Divinity School, they were required to sit on benches until they were called to the Vice Chancellor. "He called as many as would fit before him, then he gabbled something in Latin and lifted his cap." The students bowed and were dismissed. Helen was disgusted. "On the whole, it was a decidedly stupid performance." She was told the sneers of the Vice-Chancellor were a result of his being one of the die-hards who had not forgiven women for having been admitted to the university.

The most thrilling thing for Helen, always interested in architecture, was seeing the Divinity School, "a beautiful medieval hall with a stone roof, arched and groined," built in the 15th Century as a memorial to the good Duke Humphrey of Gloucester. It was exciting for the young woman from Ohio, an eager student of history, to realize it was in this spot that Latimer and Ridley had appeared to defend their heresies in the reign of Bloody Mary. And Charles I, having been driven from London, held his Parliament here.

Helen, who had been quick to participate in as much as possible at Wellesley, was much restrained during her first year at Oxford. There was a meeting for new students to hear about the clubs and have tea. "I can't see myself taking up hockey or lacross or any game at my advanced age...nor do I want to sit in a circle and read Shakespeare," she scoffed.

"Do write often," Helen implored, "and ask me anything." In answer to a previous inquiry from her father, Helen informed him that "a bowler hat is one of those flat derbies that sits down on the ears." One last parting postscript. "The Presbyterian minister's wife has called on me -- a commanding woman with a mustache."

Her thesis topic was finally resolved, so was the matter of her tutor, and Helen felt she could get on with her work at last. The thesis would deal with 17th Century women writers, specifically Clara Reeve, a leading author of the day who wrote about her time and place. Named as her tutor was Mr. Littleboy, "who proved to be a very long boy, with black hair, brown eyes, tortoise shell glasses and a pimply chin. Unprepossessing but nice." They would become good friends and later, when Mr. Littleboy was offered a fellowship in America, she would miss him.

Life settled down to a work regimen with plenty of time for teas and walks. Particularly pleasing to Helen in those first days was the weather. By the end of October it was cold and forty degrees but clear, very much like the weather at home. "Oxford is a gloriously beautiful place," she wrote enthusiastically. "High Street," she thought, "was particularly lovely; it was lined with elms whose trunks are four or five feet in diameter...on one side the colleges and their gardens, on the other the University parks with the cricket grounds etc."[2]

Her living arrangements were working out well, too, in spite of the fact that dog-loving Helen had taken on the care of the two household cats. One of the cats, a tortoise, she thought was "quite sweet;" the other, a "yellow monster" was horrible. All-in-all, however, she felt it was little enough to do in return for having her windows shut, her fire lighted and her bath heated every morning.

Politics was always a subject of conversation at home and, when the British election was held on October 29, it was of great interest. "This is a strong conservative household...even the maid voted 'conserv'." The real question of the day, everyone seemed to think, was the possibility of socialism becoming communism and therefore creating a stronger foe of Constitutionality. Helen did not think Americans realized how far radicalism had gone in England. The Conservatives considered, in 1924, that theirs was a dying cause. They did not say "if Labor comes in" but "when Labor comes in." They believed that the British Empire was a thing of the past. Helen, who had cast an absentee ballot before she left America, was eagerly awaiting the results of the coming election in the U.S. in November.

When the election results announced that Calvin Coolidge had won, Helen wrote to her family to say how fortunate it had turned out the way it had. The conservative papers in England were rejoicing at the result. They would have preferred Davis, who was thought to be a better friend to England, but Coolidge was better than the alternatives, Al Smith and William McAdoo. Both elections had been concerned with the problem of Russia; should it be recognized by Western nations now that the revolution was over?

Helen always enjoyed a good joke, even if it was on herself. One British joke that she enjoyed was told by a man who was not fond of Americans. It concerned an Englishman who was showing an American around London. The Englishman pointed with pride to the Bank of England. "Oh," said the American scornfully, "we could have built that in about three weeks with reinforced concrete." They passed the Royal Exchange, which the American claimed could have been built in New

York in two weeks. As they approached St. Paul's Cathedral the Englishman, fed up with the boorish American, looked up in surprise. "I say, I don't remember having seen that building when I came down this morning!" An English woman, overhearing the story, blinked for a minute then added, "I suppose there was a heavy fog."

While Helen wrote home about her experiences, her father, in turn wrote of family news. Sister Jane's father-in-law died and consequently she and her young family were returning to Xenia. Frequently he commented on Grandpa Hooven's growing senility, local gossip and he always commented on the magazines and clippings which he thought Helen would enjoy seeing. "Mother is doing very well with her metal work in silver and gold. It seems to me she is doing some mighty nice work." Mr. Santmyer never missed an opportunity to praise his wife. He supported her in her interests and praised her often.

"Do not think," Father wrote to his daughter, "that because you are at a distance that you are not in our thoughts...never a day goes by that you are not a subject of family conversations."

As the term drew to a close and 1924 was about to end, plans were underway for Helen's holidays to France with Adeline Aldrich.

Chapter 10

❧

Holidays in Paris

Three weeks off and one of them in Paris!   Helen and Adeline Aldrich were busy making plans for the holidays in their favorite city. After Christmas Adeline planned to go on to Berlin to visit her former roommate, now married to a young man attached to the American Embassy there. Helen was going to return to Oxford before the second term started to catch up on work that had been postponed during the search for a thesis topic.

Helen didn't want her parents to think she was being extravagant so she assured them the trip should not be expensive. She was traveling second-class, and she was planning to stay at the American University Women's Club, where the maximum charge for a room and three meals was thirty-five francs. She had already finished her Christmas shopping -- antiques for everyone, including her young brother, Phil, who was developing an interest in collecting them -- and she was about to mail them home. She hoped they would arrive safely. The shopkeepers promised they would arrive undamaged. As it turned out, some did and some did not. She requested that they send their presents to her at Oxford as they would be safer there.

Casually, in one of the letters written before she left, Helen mentioned that she had some news that she thought would please them. Houghton Mifflin, it seemed, was interested in publishing her book. *Herbs and Apples* would be published if she agreed to a few conditions. She would have to shorten the book, long books were expensive to publish, and they wanted her to agree to an option on her second book. Helen hated to cut her work, but she realized it was too long and even admitted it was dull in a few spots. Not surprised at the condition, she agreed to shorten the manuscript. She was flattered that they wanted her second book and that they even thought she could write a second book. The problem was: what would she write about? The editor would be in England in March and would arrange to see her while he was there. If she agreed to the conditions, they would sign the contract at that time. She asked Houghton Mifflin to return the manuscript to her at Oxford and she would do her best to rewrite the book before the editor met with her.

With that exciting possibility on her mind, Helen left with Adeline for The City of Light. They settled into the Club she had mentioned to her family and immediately set off on a sightseeing tour to see what they could before the museums closed. Because the museums were not equipped with electric lights, they closed at 4:00 pm. The first stop was The Grand Palais on the Champs Elysee. Helen was impressed with the sheer size of it. It covered so much space, one couldn't see much of it in an hour-and-a-half. "They exhibit absolutely everything; Mother would love it."[1] There were rooms of furniture, alcoves filled with tapestries, needlepoint, materials in new designs, jewels, pottery, vases and glorious bowls. "Then, of course, sculpture, almost all quite dreadful." But Helen admitted the paintings were mixed, all modern, but some lovely and some horrible. She liked the landscapes painted in clear bright colors and pictures of the sea. Some of the portraits were fine, "but I must admit that fat nude women predominate to an absurd extent." Although not easily shocked, Helen and Adeline "decided that picnic parties in the woods or along the seashore with no clothes whatever must be quite the thing this year."

What is Paris if one doesn't visit the shops? The stores were marvelous on such streets as the Rue Royale, the Rue de Rivoli and Rue de la Paix. "New York City is almost a country town by comparison." The women treated themselves to new made-to-order dresses, described in minute detail by Helen to her family. It was not necessary but she felt she should justify her purchase by explaining how much cheaper clothes were in Paris than at home, and if she had asked for a new dress before she left home, her mother certainly would have bought her one. They could just consider they bought her one in Paris.

The young women "attended the opera and the theater to see 'the beau monde'; went to Montmartre to see the wild life; visited the Latin Quarter where the Sorbonne is and the academies, etc." As was her custom, Helen bought a map of the city to send to her parents so they could follow her tours and see what she was referring to in her letters. She was so excited she pleaded with her mother to join her and see for herself. She found one could live in Paris cheaply. If her mother couldn't make the trip this year, maybe next year. But bring a fur coat, she cautioned. It was cold in Paris in December and she "rejoiced" in her fur coat, which she wore every day and slept under every night.

The day before Christmas Helen went to Sainte Chapelle, a little royal palace built by Louis IV in the vicinity of Notre Dame to house the relics he had brought back from the Crusades. They also went to see the Arc de Triomphe and the grave of the Unknown Soldier, where the flame burns all the time, and they visited the little Cluny Museum. "Indeed, they say you can learn everything there is to learn about the domestic life of the Middle Ages at the Cluny Museum."

Christmas Day was an unusual one for Helen. Everyone at the Club had colds so they did not go to the midnight mass, which was all right with Helen who was not Catholic. Instead they slept most of the morning had lunch, walked in the afternoon and had chocolate at La Poiret Blanche and returned to the Club for dinner. A long banquet table was set up in the large hall, and an American flag was hung over the mantle. The Club had spared no effort to make the guests feel at home.

Dinner was delicious, Helen reported, it included: chicken, turkey, with cranberries and chestnut dressing, cauliflower, salad, and a flaming plum pudding for dessert -- all served with champange.

When the Christmas festivities were over, Adeline made arrangements to go to Berlin, and Helen prepared for her return to London for a few days before continuing her work in Oxford. But "The best laid schemes o' mice and men," Robert Burns once said, "Gang aft a-gley." (Things don't always turn out the way they are planned.)

Chapter 11

❧

"Best Laid Schemes..."

During all their Christmas travels Helen had complained about French trains. The trains they took on their travels, Helen felt, left much to be desired, "they are crowded, hot and noisy and shake your head off your shoulders."[1]

Possibly she was overly critical, for she did not feel very well. In fact, she had not felt well for several days. When she finally turned an obvious shade of yellow, the doctor declared it jaundice, "a liver condition that was a common ailment among Americans in Paris." It became necessary for Helen to postpone her return to Oxford for several days. Food had always been an important part of Helen's life and now, after such fine cuisine in France, she was condemned to a diet of clear vegetable soup for three weeks. "I must say I am very irritable about it." Once beyond the clear soup, she was still restricted to no butter, no meat, no coffee or tea -- only vegetables, fruit, oatmeal and milk, Helen groaned. "I never knew how much my stomach means to me!" After a few days in bed she was released and allowed to return to England. Fortunately, the Channel was quiet after the storm.

Arriving back in Oxford, still on her meager diet, Helen wrote to her family and admitted she had been homesick at Christmas and wished for more details of the family's festivities and the little nieces. She was still feeling somewhat sorry for herself when she told them of her friend Vedder, who had just sold a poem to be published in the Christmas issue of *Life*. Though it was to appear prominently in this leading weekly magazine, the publishers only paid her fifty dollars for it. Life wasn't fair somehow.

Her manuscript had been returned by Houghton Mifflin while she was away, and she was now hard at work on revising it even though she was still not feeling up to par. She worked at the revisions in the mornings and on her thesis in the afternoons. She was wearing herself out, it seemed. In addition, she feared she would not have the revisions finished before March when Mr. Greenslet, the editor from Houghton Mifflin, was due to arrive. "I'm afraid I can't revise it to suit him and that they won't want it after all." She requested that her family not talk about her book to anyone. "It would be dreadful if it were to fall through."

Mr. Santmyer, in the meantime, wrote to Helen to try to cheer her up and encourage her. Her Christmas presents had arrived in good shape...mostly. They were concerned about her health and hoped she was feeling better. Jane's little girls, they assured Helen, were perfectly adorable and they loved her presents. Then, Father turned to politics: "This is Thrift Week throughout the country and today is Give To Others Day. Honestly, I think the nation is going 'nuts' - we are constantly being told what to celebrate and how to do it and how to behave and what to eat - our morals are constantly being looked after by self-appointed censors, etc." It is interesting to note how many things do not change!

Father reminded Helen to let him know in plenty of time if she needed more money. He suggested that if she could manage until after March 1st it would be helpful to him, "but if you need it before then let me know and I will manage to send it -- I do not want you to be embarrassed by being in need and I certainly don't want you to be humiliated by being broke..." He encouraged Helen to see Italy at term's end. It might be cheaper than living in England, and she must see it before she returned home. He agreed with Helen that it was too bad her mother could not join her on her jaunts but it was just not possible at this time. Young Phil, soon to be a student at Johns Hopkins University, was planning a trip to Europe for the summer in 1926 -- going student class with a group -- and Father could only support so much! Helen had been devoted to Phil since the day he was born. She wished she were in a position to help him financially herself, and she certainly didn't want him to be deprived of anything because of her.

The weather was frequently a topic for letters going either way across the Atlantic. Helen declared that the glorious weather in England had gone and the fog had settled in. "It's bound to be foggy, because the whole country is under water, and every time the sun comes out it draws up a mist." It was only January, but in England the primroses and the cowslips and the snowdrops were all in bloom in the garden, she informed her flower-loving mother, "and the nasturtiums and the bulbs have sprouted -- and of course the grass never ceases to be green."

"Oxford is beautiful," she repeats, "the homes are centuries old and perfectly delightful to behold, but none of them have bathrooms or even running water... the water is carried to a whole block and, what is more, often one outside the w.c. [toilet] has to serve a large group of houses. There are things to be said against medieval Oxford, as well as for it!" On the positive side, picturesque High Street never ceased to charm her with its churches and colleges and pedestrians. "Students, of course, with their gowns around their necks, ancient and decayed clergymen...[who] wear throughout the winter very hard and shiny black straw hats; nurserymaids in cap-and-cape wheeling blond and rosy children; and groups of little boys from the Magdalen Choir School scampering home in mortar boards and black gowns. The High Street is such a constant delight..."

Helen was busy planning a trip for the spring holidays. Father had written again to encourage Helen to go to Italy. She should also see Denmark, he suggested, because her mother had Danish blood as well as Irish forebears. She must also travel to Scotland and Wales and see England thoroughly. "Make the most of your holidays, and remember to send us maps and postcards."[2]

Helen assured her father that she wanted to go to Italy very much, but it was a Holy Year. Thousands of pilgrims would be there, particularly the Irish from Boston, and Helen felt it would be better to see the country another time. She, on the other hand, had thought of a bicycle trip to Cornwall for part of the vacation. Another part might include a visit to The Hague. The Lees' house guest, Miss Nicholson, knew everyone and offered to write letters of introduction for Helen. The idea had great appeal for Helen, who appreciated the finer things of life. "It would be rather fun, I think, to meet people of the upper-crust of Dutch Society," she wrote.

Though she was busy cutting the length of her book and at the same time trying to achieve some progress on her thesis, there was still time for some social fun. She apologized to her family for not having written sooner, but revising in the morning and working in the library in the afternoon leaves little time for things like tea with friends such as Adeline, a young Virginian named Jim Garrick and a young man named Anderson from Dartmouth. In spite of her long hours of hard work, however, the editor was due soon and she hadn't nearly finished copying the novel. She wrote everything by hand. "The thesis wasn't progressing very rapidly either." About the only thing she had to report to her tutor, Mr. Littleboy, was the title. But gathering so much material -- a list of 2000 novels published by women writers before 1800 -- was unbelievable. "Who would have dreamed there were so many?"

Her worries about the manuscript for Mr. Greenslet were unfounded, for on March 3rd Helen wrote, "At last I have finished revising the great work..." She felt she was ready to meet with Houghton Mifflin's representative. In the meantime, with the pressure somewhat relieved, Helen continued to form her plans for the summer holiday venture -- from the third week in June until the second week in October. She had been trying to find someone who would be a compatible traveling companion.

"There is no English person I know well enough or like well enough to travel with except Miss Lees, the younger, who is really darling -- but she is poor as Job's turkey and could only go on short trips, if at all." Helen wasn't looking forward to a long break. She didn't know anyone from home who was planning to be in England except Miss Lockwood from Wellesley. If she were to come Helen felt she could spend the summer with her. Also a friend from Xenia was planning to be abroad, it seemed, and Helen felt "she would not only be congenial but she is as poor as I am..." With the prospect of at least one friend to join her, she could look forward to the long holiday after all.

But first, there was a spring break to enjoy. Helen thought she would consider renting a punt for travel on the Thames. She had several friends with whom she might undertake such an outing. It would be fun. Father's reply to her suggestion included his understanding that a punt was simply a flat bottomed scow and punting simply pushing the scow along with a stick. "Maybe it will prove to be lots of fun," he conceded, "but I don't believe it will be very exciting unless someone falls overboard."

Helen's spring plans began to take shape. They included a London visit with Miss Lees, the older, from March 18th to April 8th at a cheap hotel, The White Hall, on Montague Street near the British Museum; then two weeks as a guest of the Mr. and Mrs. Lees in Shropshire. The young Miss Lees would remain in Oxford to oversee the spring cleaning of the house, including the chimneys. Helen lamented the fact, "I'm sorry I shall be away -- I should like to see a chimney sweep in action."

As luck would have it, those plans would not quite materialize because a letter from Mr. Greenslet informed Helen that he would be fishing in Scotland from March 17th to 22nd. If she could plan to meet him in London before the 17th of March he would receive the revised manuscript. Otherwise she could send it. Knowing it was far better to meet with the man face-to-face, she planned to give him the manuscript herself no matter what plans had to be changed.

When they met in London, Mr. Greenslet informed Helen he could not make a decision on the spot -- he couldn't give her an answer until his return from Scotland. By then he would have had time to read it. He did tell her, however, that the book was to be published in the fall, and she would be paid 10% royalty, which was usual for a first novel, he assured her.

The editor was jovial and complimentary but he warned Helen not to expect to get rich on the book. "He doesn't think it will have a very wide sale, but he cheered me up for the future." He told Helen that Houghton Mifflin had paid one female novelist $150,000 for a work published during the past fall! "I told him I could guess that it was *The Little French Girl*, of course." He told her it was the first time he had ever known a book as good as that to pay that well. (Two points, Helen noticed: one was that when he referred to a 'female novelist' it probably meant that they paid male novelists on a different basis; and second, good books usually didn't pay as well as books that were not so good. Not very encouraging to a writer like Helen Santmyer.) He also told her they wouldn't put anything about her second novel in the contract.   It would be a 'gentleman's' agreement! She was to give them first option on the book and they would want to publish it by 1926. "I haven't an idea in my head. I think it is rushing things a bit," she cried.

But the thesis still hung over Helen's head. Her work often took her to London and the British Museum. It was on one such trip that she found herself watching Lord Curzon's state funeral. George Nathaniel was the First Marquess Curzon of Kedleston, born in 1859, who became a British statesman and Viceroy of India. As she watched the procession, she strolled up The Mall to St. James Palace and reached there "in time to see a company of guards, [in] some kind of performance which I cannot explain...the guards were all in gray -- heavy gray overcoats with enormous bearskin hats as tall as the men themselves... also, a company of what I thought were horse guards (but Miss Lees tells me they are life guards) going by on horseback, glorious in their scarlet coats, steel breastplates and helmets and snow white trousers, gloves and horsehair plumes." After the procession, Helen cut across St. James Park to the Abbey to see people come out of the Cathedral. She had a place at the curb so she could see into every limousine. She saw Lloyd George, who "was unmistakable" and thought she saw Churchill and Lord Salisbury.

At her lowest ebb, Helen had written home to say she was worn out and homesick, even at her age, and had decided to go home for the summer if her parents didn't mind. She asked for their advice. Father responded as she guessed he would. "I want you to know you can come home anytime you want to come or think that it would be wise to do so." She must know they would be glad to have her for the summer. The expense wouldn't be very different, but they didn't want her to miss a chance to travel if she could, he told her.

Although she was pleased to hear his thoughts on the matter, she had already written again to say she was feeling better and was sorry she had even thought of going home. They must not worry, she was really all right. Father had already sent a draft for the equivalent of $1000 for her anticipated expenses, what ever she decided to do. Years later, there would be those who rued the fact that Helen had had no sponsor or benefactor and that it had been necessary for her to work for her living and write at the same time. Letters written during these crucial years seem to indicate Mr. Santmyer did his best to "sponsor" Helen and be her benefactor.

Helen had been invited by Cousin Caroline to spend her holidays with them in Chateauroux, but later she wrote to say she was not feeling well and it was probably better if Helen did not come. Disappointed, Helen understood that a houseguest, even a member of the family, could be a burden for a household that was beset by illness. She hoped her cousin would soon feel better. She would plan a visit another time. Then the word came. Cousin Caroline was dead! The family was shocked. No one had any idea she was so sick. What was wrong with her, everyone wanted to know? Since Helen had seen her not long before they all turned to her for the answer, but Helen had no idea either.

When she had visited her cousin in the fall, Caroline had been coughing continually, but she said it was a bronchial problem and didn't take it very seriously. Helen said Caroline had told her the doctor had advised her not to read. "She hadn't enough blood in her body to go around," he had told her, and if she read and used the brain the "general economy" suffered. They didn't know much about heart problems in 1925, but even Helen's father said he never heard of anything like that! (From the symptoms that Helen described, it may have been a heart valve problem which resulted in what we call "sudden death" today. It seems to have run in the family.)

Helen, and indeed all of the family, were concerned for Caroline's children. They had their grandmother, but their lives were never to be the same again. Would they move to Paris or return to the United States? After the shocking news about Cousin Caroline, Helen prepared to leave for her spring holiday and the visit to the Lees' home in Shropshire. "Shropshire is a delightful and heavenly place," Helen reported to her folks in Xenia, "there is a little country 18th Century church around the corner from the Lees home, looks just like what one would expect of an old English manor house." It had big square rooms, comfortably furnished.

Even though there were only two servants, the household ran so well Helen had guessed there were more. In addition to their usual chores, the servants brought the tea tray in the morning, "personally, I can think of nothing worse than tea before breakfast;" they were responsible for laying the fire and keeping it tended all day; and they even laid out nightclothes by the fire and turned the bed back each night.

Breakfast was cooked on an "alcohol contraption" on the sideboard and the family served themselves; luncheon was put on the table and served by Mrs. Lees. Dinner was an affair of state. "Evening clothes, of course, the maid holds the door open while guests enter the dining room and solemnly stands by the sideboard when she isn't waiting." The courses included: soup, meat, pudding, cheese and biscuits, served with sauterne, and finished with fresh fruit and port wine. "Then the ladies depart, while Mr. Lees sits with his port."

Mrs. Lees was a tall and gaunt woman, as Helen described her, with a beautiful voice. Mr. Lees was a much older man with gray hair, slightly stooped, a gentle man with a rather deprecating air. Both of the parents had spent half their lives in America. They returned to England because his presence was needed in the 300-year-old family business run by Mr. Lees and his brother.

The Lees made a concerted effort to show Helen their countryside, including Shrewsbury twenty miles away. It was the most medieval of all the towns Helen had seen. "Some streets are no wider than our driveway, you could easily shake hands across them." Other points of interest were the elaborate Elizabethan timbered houses with projecting stories above, a castle which Helen reported had been 18th Century-ized with windows, and the Severn River, not very wide at Shrewsbury. In Shrewsbury Helen purchased an antique Staffordshire tea set (reported for customs to be 120 years old), which would always remain one of her treasures. As promised, she continued to supply her parents with maps, postcards and snapshots of her excursions.

Upon her return from spring break, the new novelist was again busy with her thesis. "I have begun work on Clara Reeve's *Progress of Romance*, in which she mentioned almost every novel and romance written before 1785 and consequently I have to read them all, beginning with the Greek romance of the 1st Century A.D." [Most of Clara Reeve's books are out of print now but there is a book, *Oriental Tales*, World Classics, Oxford Press, 1992, which contains one of her stories: *The History of Charoba, Queen of Aegypt*.] Later, Helen's thesis, because of its length and attention to detail, would be thought of as Ph.D. quality, not BLD, but she insisted that if she was going to write a thesis, she would do it right.

In spite of the heavy workload, Helen and Miss Lees did get a chance to punt on the Thames. No one "fell overboard" as her father suggested, but Helen did suffer from an episode of palpitations. Miss Lees was so concerned that she fetched the doctor. He laughed at Helen for being startled, told her she had an "irritable heart" and ordered her to bed for a couple of days. "I don't know what he means by 'irritable' but he said it would be easily upset by over-exertion and would flutter a bit, but that it was nothing serious." Helen seemed to recover after some rest but there was no more punting.

"I thought I had quite recovered from my heart-flutter but I still feel so tired and good-for-nothing that I think I should rather come home for the summer." No one, not even Helen's father, seemed to associate Helen's flutter with Cousin Caroline's recent problem. "Would you like me to come? I would leave on June 8th." She had misgivings, as she had when she suggested going home earlier. She thought it a waste of money and ridiculous to be homesick at her age, "but I do long to see you!" She saw the doctor again and he saw nothing wrong but that she was run-down and "in a state of nervous depression." Helen was dismayed! "I'm sure I don't know why...unless it's a combination of hard work, rotten weather and dull food, and the fact that, after seeing an old Wellesley friend, I realized how lonely I have been here with no friends outside the household." She was to see the doctor once more before leaving for her holiday. He would then decide what she could do for the summer.

Helen's "heart flutter" suggests she may have had what is known today as a mitral valve prolapse. It is frequently caused by rhuematic fever or, as Helen had experienced, an infection with a high fever. Not much was known about valve problems until the 1980s and 1990s. For years it was thought to be psychosomatic -- a woman's disease -- but when men began to seek help for the symptoms, they discovered it was a legitimate heart problem. Many people have it in varying degrees, and sometimes it causes little or no trouble. However, it can be progressive and can become life threatening in some situations.

The doctor saw nothing wrong at that point and plans were made to go ahead with the tour of the English countryside: Chepstrow to Bristol, Bristol to Bath, then down the coast of Devon and Cornwall, back along the south coast, stopping for a week or so on the way back to London via Salisbury and Winchester. By this time Helen had discovered that so many of her friends were expected to be in England during the summer that her fears of being alone were unfounded. Now, it seemed, there were so many friends visiting in England that she didn't think she would have time to see them all! KB and Ella were arriving on the same boat. Helen was to contact Vedder, and they would meet in Plymouth. Miss

Pendleton and Miss Lockwood were recruiting for Wellesley and planned to see Helen while they were in town. She was beginning to look forward to the long summer after all.

Chapter 12

❧

The Summer of
Herbs and Apples

Helen finally received the long-awaited contract from Houghton Mifflin. In those days the use of a literary agent wasn't a common practice. Young writers were pretty much at the mercy of the publishing firm and hoped they would be treated well. Helen was no exception. Glad to have someone interested in publishing her book, she signed on the dotted line.

"It seems fairly simple -- it provides for all possible and improbable contingencies, such as destruction by fire, etc. and what must be done when the copyright expires and all that sort of thing. Of course ten per cent seems a small royalty, but I think that is what they pay at first -- and you mustn't think the other ninety per cent is profit for the publisher, because it isn't. Expenses of paper, printing, cloth and binding are high -- it costs about twenty cents to bind a book, or did when I was at Scribners -- and the retail book seller gets books at a great discount (thirty per cent generally, or more if he buys in quantities).

"The publisher's profit is really very small -- and so uncertain because the public taste is unreliable. Every book by a new author is a gamble."[1] When one considers the fact that books in 1925 sold for about two dollars, or even less sometimes, it was certain Helen would not become wealthy from the sales of *Herbs and Apples*.

It has been said of *Herbs and Apples* that some readers were more impressed with the "quiet perfection of this gemlike period piece"[2] because it more clearly manifested Helen's genius than her monumental "*..And Ladies of the Club*." Considering the fact that the author was only twenty-five and had barely started what was to be a long life, she depicted "a wonderfully evocative memory of youth's dreams and yearnings."[3]

The novel concerns a group of young women who go to college together during World War I and remain together in New York City for a few years while they pursue their individual careers, looking for early success. The protagonist, whose father is a physician it is interesting to note, is based on Helen. The book is admittedly semi-autobiographical, providing insight into the woman who would later become a famous old lady. *Herbs and Apples* was written from the heart because Helen had a story she wanted to tell.

Mr. Greenslet had written from the U.S. to say that no more revisions were necessary, but "the book proved to be longer than they thought and it would cost so much to print it from plates that they are going to set it up in Linotype. The old skinflint! It means I shan't have the chance of reading proofs... it also means they don't expect to sell many copies as you can't print and reprint from Linotype as you can from plates." But then he had told Helen all along that they didn't expect to sell many.

Helen was glad that the book was finished, for her "flutter" began to plague her. The doctor made arrangements for her to enter a London nursing home for a week of rest before she started her summer touring. Finally feeling rested and fit, she was entertained by Miss Lockwood and Miss Pendleton in London and showed them the sights of Oxford. Then with Vedder, Ella and KB, she traveled to Kenilworth, Stratford-on-Avon to see Shakespeare's home and theater, and to Warwick to see Warwick Castle, the remains of which were unchanged since the days of the king-maker Cromwell did not make the Parliamentarian stronghold uninhabitable after England's Civil War.

Returning to London, Helen became ill once more and, this time, she was ordered to Harrowgate for three weeks. Harrowgate was a well known health spa located, fortunately, in an interesting part of England, on the moors near York. Helen feared it would be expensive because it was known that royalty frequented the baths. She wrote to her father for more money as she really had no choice. Doctor Simpson, her specialist, insisted there was no other way. She was so run down, it seemed, that if she did not go for a cure at Harrowgate, she would not be well enough to finish her research and would be forced to go home!

She hated the idea of going off alone, and it was with great sadness that she said good-bye to Ella, who was now off to Paris. Ella wasn't happy about traveling alone, either, and she offered to stay at Harrowgate with Helen. Helen wouldn't hear of it; she couldn't let her friend make such a sacrifice. Returning to her little hotel near the baths, Helen had barely settled in when Ella appeared. She just couldn't leave Helen sick and alone for three weeks.

In the initial examination upon her arrival at Harrowgate, it was revealed that Helen was considerably underweight and had low blood pressure. Other than that she was healthy. Dr. Simpson prescribed visits to the mineral baths each day, massages, a strict diet, rest and "drinking that vile tasting water." It was definitely toxemia, he told her. The heart muscle had been poisoned by a streptacoccus. Today's cardiologists would probably diagnose it differently, but Helen had the best advice England had to offer at the time.

Ella didn't have to participate in Helen's regimen, but she joined her for the baths and massages which were beneficial to anyone. Going to the spa was not like going to a hospital, but it still was not what the two women had planned for their summer holiday. However, they were both committed to making the most of it while Helen recovered. In the first place, it was a beautiful location and, using Harrowgate as the hub, they could take off in many directions for day trips around the moors. The weeks passed happily enough as Helen regained her strength, at least for the moment, and it seemed as though she and Ella saw everything but the Bronte's house. To make matters even better, it was not nearly as expensive as Helen had anticipated even if the Royal family members did go there, and Helen did not need the extra money her father had sent.

It was Father who wrote the news to Helen. "...am prepared to announce that Houghton Mifflin published *Herbs and Apples* on August 28th; we expect the first copies to reach Xenia this week." He continued cautiously, "If the press deigns to notice it in any way at any time, I shall send any notice I see -- be it praise or damning." He couldn't help adding, "...rough stuff is good for one -- it develops character."

Friends were asking about the book and said they were planning to buy them. Even Mrs. G___ told him she was buying some to send to friends in China. Warily, her father continued, "I am wondering if there is anything in that book that is going to disagree with Mrs. G___." Helen's response to his concern was intended to put his mind at ease, "...some of the people may think some of the townspeople in it are drawn from life and be annoyed -- they weren't."

Miss Elwell was the first in Xenia to buy it, but Helen's childhood friend, Mildred Wright, was the first in Xenia to read *Herbs and Apples*. The book seemed to be selling well, Mr. Santmyer told his daughter, and he "was most proud to see the family name on the book cover." Mother was the first member of the family to read it, "to her great pride and satisfaction," Helen's father related. "The public is beginning to know what she knew all the time." Her mother wrote to say, "It's a good book -- I like it and I'm pleased with it and very pleased with you... and that's the truth."

The *Ft. Worth Star Telegram* judged it "Richly Poignant."

"An old-fashioned story tempered by a modern...consciousness," declared *The Cleveland Plain Dealer*.

"A sure touch that charms...leisurely, lyrical descriptions of small town life and the Ohio countryside," reported *Publishers Weekly*.

Everyone agreed, Helen must continue to be a writer. "I really think great achievement is possible from you...if you persist and strive." As fathers will, he cautioned again. "In our family it has been a gift to dream fine dreams and a family weakness to be unable, by persistence and sustained effort, to overcome inertia...don't let talent die for lack of exercise." In the excitement of the moment those words made no more impact than the buzzing of a fly.

As her family wrote congratulations and praise, Helen wrote to them, "No doubt by this time you have read my book -- I hope you like it, somewhat at least." Again, she assured them that no one in the book was a portrait of anyone except her old Wellesley friends, Eli and Monty. Helen still had not received a copy from Houghton Mifflin nor had they even told her when it would be out. She was to get twelve complimentary copies from the publisher, but if she didn't get them soon everyone she intended to give them to would already have a copy, including Grandpa Hooven who was mad because he had to read a borrowed one. He was proud of Helen and he wanted his own signed copy from her.

The cover on the book, Helen thought, was dreadful, but she thought the dust jacket was nice. Unfortunately the book was full of typographical errors which Helen felt was her fault because she didn't get a chance to read the proofs.

Helen was on edge to see if the book would be reviewed and by whom. She knew Houghton Mifflin had spent very little money in publicizing it, but reviews were crucial to its successful sales. If it were reviewed, would the reviews be favorable? "I'd rather be damned than ignored," she insisted. She had recently met an East Indian, referred to as Tink, who worked for the New York Times, and he wanted to review it. The problem was that he didn't review novels and the paper might not allow him to do it.

She had met Tink, a friend of Vedder's, shortly after she left Harrowgate. He had invited the two young women to have dinner with him and his friend, Ridgely Torrence -- from Xenia! They accepted the invitation to dinner in Twickenham, outside London, and the two men showed them the sights of Twickenham, as well as Richmond and Cheswick, in grand style. They saw the place where Alexander Pope is buried, the gardens of York Palace where Queen Anne was born, and the castle where Queen Elizabeth died. They enjoyed a fine view of the Thames Valley, went to hear a band concert and had tea. All-in-all, a most enjoyable day. They parted with plans for the gentlemen to join the ladies on Tuesday for their trip to Wincester.

Later Ridgely and Tink took Helen and Vedder out to celebrate the publication of *Herbs and Apples*; when the evening was cut short, they insisted they had to do it again -- properly! Helen and Ridgely saw each other regularly although she insisted he was a "hopeless nut." She had to admit, however, that he had a good sense of humor so there was hope. The real problem with Ridgely seemed to be the fact that he didn't know what he wanted to do "when he grew up." Helen knew what she wanted to do. Meanwhile, they had a good time together. The future would take care of itself.

As it happened, the young poet left England abruptly and sailed on the Cunard Line's R.M.S. Aquitania. He wrote to Helen that he had wanted to call her before he left, "but such a turmoil boiled up around me I found it was too late...before I knew it I ran down to Southhampton this morning and bought a ticket on the dock, half an hour before the boat went to sea, and am now nearing Cherbourg. It seems too bad not to have had one more evening with you -- one at least! But I find myself today already planning a return. In fact, I could wish myself ashore... it's rather silly, my restlessness, I was very well off before embarking, but I seemed to want to go. Now I seem to want to stay."[4] He felt it had been some kind of lesson for him and he would regret his impulsive action. "How charming it was the other night. I found myself in town the very next night at a loss because we were not again together at dinner."[5]

Helen reminded herself that she had always insisted she would not marry and, therefore, could not be involved with any man. (In addition, Ridgely Torrence was a married man, known to like the ladies.) Helen didn't realize how much she had come to value his friendship. Once more she buried herself in her work. She accepted the disappointment, but did she ever forget?

Chapter 13

❦

Going Home

Helen threw herself into the new term totally committed to finishing the thesis. Seldom had a student put so much effort into a Bachelor of Literature Degree, but Helen didn't know how to write by half-measures. She returned often to London to work in the British Museum, "the more I am in London the more I love it, in spite of the weather, the dirt and the miserable food."[1]

During the months of intense work, the reviews of her book began to arrive. Mr. Santmyer sent his daughter a copy of the review by author and noted newsman for the *Baltimore Sun*, H.L.Menken. Menken was known for his acerbic style and sharp criticism and when Helen read the review she was delighted, "...at least he didn't pan it!"

Her father also forwarded a letter and enclosed reviews from a Harvard professor, whose son would become a presidential advisor. Arthur Schlesinger, a fellow Xenian, had been interested in Helen's career and wrote to Mr. Santmyer. "I am sending herewith two reviews of your daughter's book which may have escaped your notice. Although I have not yet read her book myself, I hope soon to do so, and meantime I am proud to share in the glory which comes to all Xenians and former Xenians because of her notable first effort in the field of literature."[2]

Helen, in turn, sent her father a review from the January issue of the *New Republic* which had come to her attention. "The pattern of a woman's life has ever been a lure to the pen of the novelist. Miss Santmyer is lacking in the ability to sift her material so as to make it sustain her theme, and the narrative drags accordingly. Her backgrounds also are uneven. Her Tecumseh, in its haze of golden dust, its fields and hillsides, is wholly vivid and beautiful. Her New York is drab and flat. And be it said in mournful candor, her college atmosphere is juvenile and dreary. Yet scattered through this oddly compounded book are passages of a breath-taking delicacy and poignancy..."[3] The townspeople, too, had been most receptive. "We gals of the Woman's Club are pleased with the book,"[4] they wrote to Helen. Friends showered her with cables and letters of congratuations.

Father wrote, "You're very fortunate to have this first book published and received so well. Don't let the bad reviews disturb you," he continued, "just use them to profit by and make good the confidence of those who believe in you...first books usually don't make much money but of course later books always stimulate the sales of all that went before."

For a first book it had been noticed by the best of publications, now if it would just make some money for Helen! She was quite encouraged when she received the first accounting statement from Houghton Mifflin in November. Mr. Greenslet said it represented only one month's sales, a total of 1097 copies at $2.50 per copy. That would mean the impressive sum of $274.25 for Helen! The royalty check would not be sent out until March, however. In the meantime, she took pen in hand and once more wrote to her father. "I hate like anything to ask for it, but..." It was her fervent dream that her book would succeed and she wouldn't have to ask her family for money again. Maybe she could even help them a little by helping with Phil's expenses.

Letters home from Helen reported "nothing to write about;" it was just hard work and she was exhausted. She was also becoming disillusioned with the English educational system. "I must say, the more

I survey this institution with a cold and critical eye, the more I think we Americans have been too willing to accept the English valuation of his system. It works for the best man, but I can't see that it works at all for the average man. And as for women, it isn't adapted for one out of a hundred."

The hard work continued week after week. Finally, in November, Helen was summoned by Miss Rook, her new supervisor. Miss Rook went over Helen's thesis and declared she thought it would do with some minor editing. By the early part of December in 1926, the second part of the thesis was due. Helen was beginning to see the light at the end of the long tunnel. Her work was almost finished. Now came the period of waiting to have the thesis accepted for the degree.

The long-distance exchange of Christmas presents occurred for the third year. Helen was anxious to enjoy the next one in Xenia, in the warm company of her family. New Years came and went. It seemed that 1927 would be a memorable year. To begin with, in March Helen enjoyed a dinner dance given in honor of the Rhodes Scholars by the Vicountess Astor at 4, St. James Square. The *London Times* wrote an account of the affair and listed the royal family members and notables that also attended. Helen admitted she could write "at epic length" about the event. "The aristocracy, youth, beauty, and wealth of England was there. The house...is a huge and magnificent place -- the sort of house I had never been in before until it had been turned into a museum." The dance was well managed and no women were left on the sidelines. The Prince of Wales was there, and so was Sir James Barrie, the playwright, and the Baldwins (he was editor of the Times). All in all, it was a thrilling experience for the young woman from Xenia.

In June her thesis would be finished even if, as Miss Rook believed, her examiner didn't realize how much work had gone into it. Fortunately, she had friends in London who were also working at the British museum so she had "some human intercourse" during the long tedious weeks. There was an art exhibit of six hundred of Sargent's paintings, and an occasional tea or luncheon, but compared to other times in her life there were few diversions while she waited for acceptance and the final examination necessary for the degree. She was beginning to make plans for her return, however, and wrote to say she was definitely planning to return by Cunard Line, especially since her friend Roy Ridley had a friend among the officials and swore he could get Helen a cheap passage. "I may come second class on one of the big boats instead of on one of the one-class boats, just for the sake of making a quicker trip." She promised that as soon as she knew when she would be able to leave she would let her family know "at once, you can be sure of that!"

But there was much more waiting to be done before Helen could leave for home. Mr. Nichole, her examiner, was in the midst of checking all the references of her thesis in the Bodleian to make sure they were correct. Because she had used so many sources it was taking an extraordinarily long time.

The waiting was finally over in late 1927 when the thesis was accepted. Helen passed her examination. She could expect to receive her degree later when she was back in the United States. Returning home, she found herself at what seemed like the apex of her career. She had a new prestigious degree, she had a recently published book to her credit, she had a second book already sought by Houghton Mifflin and she was beginning to realize income from her writing. Things were finally coming together for her. The fame she sought for so long seemed a real possibility. Things just couldn't get much better! It was with great joy and plans for the future that she returned to the security of her home and family to seek a deserved rest.

Part I

(1927-1953)

The Years Between

Chapter 14

❧

The Mac Dowell Colony and Other Places

After three years away from Xenia, there was much catching up to be done by Helen and her family. How her brother had matured! He was a boy when she left and now he was a man. Her nieces, too, had changed. They were no longer babies, but active, lovely little girls that Helen adored. Mother was glad to have Helen under her roof once more. She enjoyed being able to fuss over her. Father finally had a chance to get a first hand account of Helen's travels and enjoy her peregrinations vicariously, at least. Helen could see what changes had occurred in the old house since she went away – her mother's studio, the refinished floors and furniture, and her mother's well-crafted metal work, all the things they had written about.

When all of Helen's baggage finally arrived it was time to show off the antique china, the books, prints, linen, etc., that she had acquired while she was in England and France. Much of it she kept for herself, but there were treasures to be meted out to family members as well. Homecoming was like Christmas only better.

The town welcomed their famous writer home, too. Friends and family came from far and wide to see Helen and, through the haze of parties and luncheons and teas, there was a faint remembrance of those dreams of fame she had had many years ago. But if one book did not make a famous writer, there was another book to be written soon for Houghton Mifflin and hopefully some poems and stories. First, she needed a rest and a chance to recover her health now that she was home. There would be time enough to get back to work.

Invitations began to come in from Wellesley classmates. Helen's tenth reunion at Wellesley was coming up, and they were all anxious to make plans to see her at Alumnae Weekend. In June 1928 Helen went to Dublin, New Hampshire to visit Vedder for a few days before they drove on to Wellesley to meet with Monty, Tim, and Lene. There would be breakfast with Miss Lockwood, the parade, the President's Reception, etc., and then the graduation day celebration. Reunion was always something Helen looked forward to and she returned as often as she could, but this year -- author of a new book and fresh from Oxford -- it would be especially notable.

After Wellesley, Vedder and Helen drove to Cape Cod to visit with Eli, then on to see KB, whose mother had a house in Woods Hole. The weather was glorious. Helen had a wonderful time, but she had been away from her family for so long, she wanted to go home in spite of the beastly heat wave Ohio was experiencing. Before going home, however, she wanted to stop in New York City for a few days to see Hefty and Speck, more long-time friends from her Wellesley days. Also, she wanted to drop in on Mr. Bridges at Scribners and Sons. Mr. Bridges was very cordial. They had a long conversation and he wished her well.

In April of 1929 Helen's second book, *The Fierce Dispute*, was published. Her brother, Phil, upon receiving his copy at John's Hopkins University, quickly wrote to thank her and chide her a bit. "I looked through the book twice and couldn't find any pictures. I hate it when I have to create images in my own mind."[1] Also, he told her he was sorry to find it was not a murder mystery... he loved mysteries. In addition, he thought her heroine was psychotic and should be in a mental institution, and the book, he noted, was very short. How Helen must have laughed at his critique!

For the first time she located her story in Xenia and this novel, she insisted, was pure fiction. It involved three generations of women living in a big house on the edge of town, a grandmother who felt her daughter had disgraced the family when she married an Italian musician who subsequently left her and their baby penniless, the daughter who lived in her romantic past, and the granddaughter who loved them both and struggled to unite them. Finally, "the three come together to share a haunting, uplifting revelation of love."[2]

The Publisher's Note in the reprinted 1987 edition of *The Fierce Dispute* quotes Weldon A. Kefauver, the editor who first read and recommended the publication of Helen's famous third novel "...*And Ladies of the Club*", who states: "*The Fierce Dispute* has a very special quality, and it introduces many of the themes that she was to treat at the end of her career. Her statement of these themes in this early novel is perhaps even clearer than it was later."[3]

Dr. Maxwell Simpson, Helen's doctor in London, wrote her a nice letter of thanks for his copy of *The Fierce Dispute*. He added that he believed she would be wise to continue teaching, "especially in such congenial conditions [and] there was no need to abandon your creative pen."[4] Teaching would provide "a sense of independent detachment from financial care,"[5] long a concern of Helen's.

Helen did heed Doctor Simpson's advice, and for a second time chose to teach for a year at Xenia High School to provide that "detachment from financial care," until something else developed. In the meantime she would hone her craft.

In the summer of 1930, Helen applied and was accepted at the MacDowell Colony, a writer's retreat in Peterborough, New Hampshire founded by the composer Edward MacDowell for the benefit of creative people who had proven themselves and needed a sanctuary. It wasn't far from Vedder's home in Dublin, so the published poet applied and joined Helen there for a summer of writing. Private, single cottages tucked in the cool woods of New Hampshire, with meals delivered to the door and the camaraderie of sixty other creative people. Twelve composers, six artists and forty writers, including poets, playwrights, novelists and essayists were all overseen by the MacDowells. Life at the Colony made an ideal living arrangement for Helen Santmyer. In the eight weeks, the most time allotted to a resident, she started on a new book, wrote some stories intended for sale to magazine publications, and made wonderful new friends.

Halfway through the eight week period Helen wrote to her family to tell them she had finished the first draft of her new book which would become *Farewell Summer*, and was beginning to write it. "But I cannot finish it in a month no matter how hard I try." *Farewell Summer*, again located in Xenia, is concerned with a young girl who finds love, innocent and elusive, and learns over one summer that even if one sees sorrow ahead, the course of events cannot be altered.

Helen, of course, needed money to pay the rest of her board bill and she needed money for the trip home. As usual, she hated to ask for it. She had some money left but not enough. However, she had some stories intended for sale to magazine publishers if she could only find one that wanted to buy them. If worse came to worst, she could sell her treasured old copy of *Through the Looking Glass*, bought while she was in England, for she knew it had increased in value. Fortunately, Father provided the money. It did not become necessary for her to part with Lewis Carroll's classic.

In the group at the colony that summer of 1930, were names that later became famous: Edgar Arlington Robinson, William Rose Benet, and Thornton Wilder (also from Ohio) who would be compared to Helen as a midwestern writer. Included in the group was the playwright Daniel Reed who was to have three plays staged [one of his own and two dramatizations of novels by Julia Peterkins]. If that were not enough to make him interesting, he was a great friend of Ridgely Torrence!

Helen enjoyed the company of Thornton Wilder, and they developed a lasting friendship. "The shine he has taken to us is very flattering, especially since we did not go out of our way to encourage it..." There were walks in the woods, sodas in the village, and long talks in which they discussed their works in progress. "If he writes all the ideas he has had since he has been here, he'll be a very busy writer."

As the summer drew to a close, Helen cleared out her little studio and held a tea dance. She borrowed a Victrola and made lots of iced tea and lemonade. Wilder brought the bottle of applejack to liven up the lemonade and evoke joyous cries from the men. Prohibition in the United States in the 1930s meant no liquor for parties was allowed. "Now," Helen complained, "I am left with the chore of disposing of the tell-tale empty applejack bottle in the raspberry bushes."

One of the more memorable parties was Thornton Wilder's farewell party in Helen's honor, a final gesture of friendship.

After leaving the MacDowell Colony, Vedder and Helen drove to Woods Hole for a few days, then to Schenectady, then to Lime Rock to visit Hefty for a weekend then, if the car lasted, they would head west for Ohio. Soon after her return to Xenia, Helen was faced with the greatest change in her life! The Great Depression, having started on Wall Street in 1929, was spreading to all corners of the country, including Xenia. The early 1930s were very dark, indeed. Along with many other companies, The R.A. Kelly Company closed its doors for the last time. Mr. Santmyer found himself out of a job. The only prospect for another one seemed to be on the West Coast. The Santmyers, after three generations, sold the white house on Third Street and moved, Helen included, to Orange County, California.

It was an exciting adventure. The climate in California was glorious, even if the Santmyers did miss the snow in winter and the brilliant colors of the fall, and there were many nice people, some of them from Greene County, Ohio.

But the draw toward home grew stronger every year. After three years Mr. Santmyer, his health failing, retired from business. The family moved happily back to Xenia, to an unknown future. Now it was time for Helen to carry her share of life's burden and help those two who had helped her for so many years.

Chapter 15

❧

Cedarville College

Upon the return of the Santmyers to Ohio from California in 1935, it was necessary for Helen to assume the responsibility of caring for her aging parents.

She continued to try to sell her writing. In the spring of 1933, she sent some written sketches to *The Atlantic Monthly* for their consideration. The rejection letter from the editor was disappointing but encouraging: "I have done very wrong in keeping these sketches so long. My only excuse is the very genuine interest which we felt in them. Delightfully written, they are so expressive of an age that is past never to return that I really hated to part with them." Evidently reminiscences were out of fashion at that point and the magazine couldn't use them. But the letter continued: "I have considered the idea of taking one, and letting the others go, but they really belong together, and one needs the three to bring back in full perspective the world you describe."[1] The words were flattering but money would have been more helpful.

Helen needed that freedom from care that Dr. Simpson had written about years ago. She needed a job. Given few choices, she accepted an offer from Cedarville College, a small Presbyterian college in a small town eight miles north of Xenia. She would teach English and hopefully still have time to do some writing of her own. It would only be for a few years, she thought, until the Depression was over.

Because Helen had no car and didn't drive, she considered commuting on the little bus that ran between Xenia and Cedarville. Unfortunately, the bus schedule did not accommodate Helen's teaching schedule and it was decided, sadly, that it would be more practical for them to live in Cedarville. After a few years, Helen could acquire a position more fitting to her experience.

An apartment was found on Main Street in the middle of Cedarville, one flight above the dry cleaning establishment. It wasn't like the house on Third Street but it certainly was convenient. It was surrounded by shops which would provide the daily necessities, and, since it was only about four blocks from the college at the top of the hill, Helen could walk to work. In 1932 Cedarville was a nice friendly town. It boasted a bank, three grocery stores, a bakery, a hardware store, an ice cream parlor, a drug store with a soda fountain, plus a dry goods store, a movie theater and an opera house. It was a thriving farming community. In those years before everyone had a car and went out of town to shop in neighboring cities and malls, everyone went to town on Saturday night to do their shopping, have a soda, go to the movies and visit with their friends and neighbors. Cars and trucks were parked along the curbs, where one could see and be seen.

Cedarville also had a wonderful library. It was built by Andrew Carnegie, a Scottish immigrant who believed in education and spent much of his vast fortune building libraries in small towns around the United States in order to make books available to everyone. The people of Cedarville made the most of that opportunity and used the library, not only on Saturday nights, but every chance they had.

Cedarville was smaller than Xenia, which was the county seat. It did not have many social advantages offered by the larger community, but Cedarville was a pleasant little town. The apartment, on the other hand, was dark and dreary. Facing Main Street and running from back to front, with no windows on the sides, it contained only four rooms -- living room, eat-in kitchen, two bedrooms and a bath. Understandably, it had little light and the large pieces of furniture which had been moved from the big house in Xenia did nothing to make the apartment more cheerful.

The Santmyers rented the apartment from the Huey family in 1935 and paid fifteen dollars a month for the privilege. Even when the Chaplins bought the building in 1946, they could not raise the rent because of government-decreed rent control. The Chaplins also owned the dry cleaning store downstairs. It was the job of their son, Earl, to collect the rent. He noticed that the apartment was cold in the winter, but the Santmyers would turn the heat down low and wear coats or jackets to keep warm. To some they seemed "cheap and stingy." To others of that era, they were considered "thrifty." Wearing coats or jackets to conserve fuel, many people believed, meant "waste not, want not." The Santmyers had always been careful not to waste and now in the middle of the Great Depression it was even more important.

Mrs. Elwood Shaw, whose husband was a professor at Cedarville College with Helen, served as Helen's typist and often went to the apartment to work. Because Helen wrote everything in longhand, it was Mrs. Shaw's job to type any manuscripts for submission to publications. She typed stories and poems and some of the sketches which would later be used in "...*And Ladies of the Club*." Mrs. Shaw remembers the apartment had little light and was not very cheery but she doesn't remember being cold when she worked there. She didn't think of the Santmyers as being deprived in any way.

Helen did not make a large salary, about one hundred dollars per month, and her contract stated it could be decreased if the college found it fiscally necessary. Even at that, her salary should have been adequate to support three people in that economy for they lived modestly and Helen's brother and sister contributed to the support of their parents. The Santmyers did not live in the style to which they had been accustomed in the halcyon days of Xenia, but they were certainly not destitute.

What the parents did through the long hours of those endless days, we can only surmise. We know they did not participate in any community activities, and it appears they made no friends. Mrs. Santmyer, who had always been an avid gardener in Xenia, had no place for a garden in Cedarville. Now, she concentrated on her painting and metal work. She also had the responsibility of cooking and keeping the apartment clean. Mr. Santmyer had time to read and smoke his pipe. They visited with the family in Xenia often and the family, in turn, came frequently to Cedarville. The grandchildren ran through the rooms and helped Grandmother bake cookies and cakes. They were allowed to lick the bowls. Helen, always good with little children, would get down with them at their level and seem to become one of them as she played. The little children brought a good deal of sunshine into that otherwise drab household.

Compared to the lively and interesting years of her youth, Helen's life was not challenging. Her days were filled with classes and meetings. Cedarville College was delighted to have someone with Helen Santmyer's credentials and they tried to accommodate her as best they could. But Helen had never been one to tolerate stupidity or ineptness with much grace and patience. She did her best with those students who did not show much interest in her literature courses, but she was quick to point out their shortcomings with a rather acerbic tongue. More often, however, her students found that she was distant, aloof, unapproachable and polite but not friendly.

On the other hand, when Helen found a bright deserving student, she would go to any lengths to help. In the mid-1940s, James Wisecup, a recent graduate of Cedarville High School, a baseball player and, admittedly, a would-be ladies man, enrolled in Cedarville College in order to play on their baseball team and to date girls. He hadn't foreseen "literature with Miss Santmyer." He was flunking out by the second semester and Santmyer's failing mark was the final blow. He made arrangements to go to see her.

A bit fearful of the formidable Miss Santmyer, he gathered his courage and faced the inevitable. Helen smiled at the young man standing before her, perhaps enjoying the fact that he thought she was so unapproachable. She sat on the edge of the desk as she often did, her feet not touching the floor and her legs held stiffly together. Her students wondered how she could sit like that for so long and not move. "You're a bright boy, Mr. Wisecup," she told him, "and you can do much better work than you have been doing. Do you realize how foolish you are? You are working at two jobs in order to pay your tuition, yet you throw it all away by not applying yourself to your studies." Helen had always related well to children, and on occasion her motherly instincts became evident.

Jim came from a modest background and was the first of his family to go to college. He was an only child and his mother was very proud of him. He didn't want to disappoint her. Jim wanted to know what he could do and asked if it was too late.

Helen wanted to know how much he wanted to succeed. "I'll do anything it takes," he told her.

Helen offered to tutor the young student until he had made up the exams and papers. If, upon re-examination, he could make the grade, she would pass him. Together they worked every free minute. Helen took her responsibility seriously, and urged Jim to hang in there. Not only did James Wisecup graduate from Cedarville College, he went on to earn a Masters Degree in education and a Ph.D. as well. He had a long and successful career as an educator and administrator, and he credited Helen Santmyer with saving him from failure.

Helen was now considered an old maid school teacher. At fifty, she didn't feel old but she dressed the part and played the role she had designed for herself. Once a stylishly dressed young traveler who loved color and followed the fashions, she is now remembered by her students as one who dressed in shapeless dresses of drab earthy colors, "old woman's shoes" and most unremarkable hats. With her hair pulled back severely, no make up and more aloof than ever. "She expected perfection," one student complained. Another admitted "she really knew her literature and she never used any notes in her classes," but few of Helen's students remember her fondly. She did not allow them to see the sharp wit and ready humor that lay behind the facade she had created. It was as she had written when she was very young, she needed "externals" to show the world and behind which she could hide. Only a select few knew she had a truly caring nature.

One of the assignments she gave her class was to write an essay on any subject of their choice. A rather shiftless young man who had done little preparation decided to write on baseball. He didn't know much about baseball but, he assumed, neither did the old lady. He handed in the paper, errors and all, and waited for the results. Helen corrected the grammar and the spelling, then, to his chagrin, she corrected his baseball facts as well. He would never know what a laugh she got from the incident. She was an avid baseball fan, she loyally followed the Cedarville College team and was a devoted lifelong fan of the Cincinnati Reds.

During World War II, Helen received a letter from a service man who was a former student of hers at Cedarville College now far from home. He wrote about being lonely. Helen knew about that. He was afraid sometimes and missed home. Helen knew about that. He remembered how kind she had been to him when he was at Cedarville. The things she taught him, he found, stayed with him. He had learned to appreciate books, even poetry, and during the years spent far from home that knowledge had been a comfort to him. He wanted to thank her. There is no record of what happened to the young soldier, but forty years later that letter remained with Helen's memories and papers. She had touched a mind.

So the years in Cedarville stretched from a few into many and Helen continued to settle for what she had. Success would not be hers. As long as she had receptive minds, she was willing to stay at the college. Besides, She had a friend -- one with whom she could exchange ideas, who was almost as educated as she was, and in whom she could confide. In 1927, Helen had met Mildred Sandoe at the public library in Xenia where Mildred worked and Helen borrowed books. They had a meeting of the minds. Mildred thought Helen was brilliant and sophisticated; Helen thought Mildred intelligent and a good listener.

On that basis the friendship grew. It became a habit for Mildred to stop by the Main Street apartment each evening and pick up Helen to go for a ride. Besides traveling the county roads, it gave Helen a chance to have a cigarette and stop to have a drink at some out-of-the-way place or nearby city. Prohibition had been repealed in 1932. Helen was a devoted daughter, a dedicated teacher and a god-fearing Presbyterian, but she smoked cigarettes and drank straight bourbon -- not considered acceptable behavior in Cedarville. Local people often gossiped about Helen's behavior, frequently not knowing fact from fiction. Helen didn't care what people thought, at least people she didn't know, but if the college found out she could lose her job.

It was during these years, between her education and work in the East and the years of retirement and success which were to follow, that Helen wrote notations for what would become part of her best seller, "...And Ladies of the Club." At night, alone in her room, she wrote verbal pictures of family and friends and their daily lives in Ohio long ago and sketches of her beloved Xenia, which would become Ohio Town. She had a remarkable gift. All that she read and saw she remembered; all that she remembered she was able to relate to her readers in every detail. She never needed to do research for her book. She only needed to verify dates from cemeteries and county records.

She lived in her writing. All the niceties of her past that she could no longer enjoy were hers. She did not write with an agent or a publisher or a market in mind. She wrote from her heart. She had something to say and in saying it she found escape from her real life. It can be assumed that during the 17 years spent in Cedarville, Helen lived more with her fictional people and places than with reality. In May 1939, Wellesley's Purple Page included news from Helen: "Santy Santmyer is near her old home in Xenia, teaching twenty odd hours a week-- everything in the English Department and Latin -- also acting as Dean at present. She has finished another manuscript. When there is time, she runs down to Cincinnati to see Katherine Cornell or the Lunts and "occasionally she reads a book ... Lucky girl"![2] But in May 1941, 'Santy' Santmyer wrote to

Wellesley's *Purple Page*: "There really isn't enough that is interesting in my life to write fifty words about. I'm still teaching English at Cedarville College and trying to behave like a Dean of Women -- not too easy for me."[3]

Helen's life had changed in the last twenty years, and many of her old college friends had faded from her present existance. Some had died. With dismay, she read of the death of her friend, poet and noted playwright for Black theater, Fredrick Ridgely Torrence. The obituary related the facts that Torrence had attended Miami University and transferred to Princeton University but left it without earning a degree. While writing, he had worked in New York City as an editor and librarian, often returning to Xenia. He had been special to Helen.

The long years in Cedarville were brought to a close by the college. The Presbyterians had sold the college to a private group who in turn sold the facility to the Baptists in 1953. A whole new regime began. The Baptists sent around a paper which all the faculty were expected to sign. It stated that the faculty member would not smoke or drink and would believe every word of the Bible in the literal sense. Helen said she could not agree to those conditions, and she would not sign such a statement. She refused. In the end it didn't matter for the Baptists fired all the Presbyterian faculty anyhow. Helen Santmyer, who had been a professor of Latin, Dean of Women and head of the English Department, was out of a job. The years of exile from Xenia were ended. The Santmyers were going home.

Part V

(1953-1986)

Success...The Final Years

Chapter 16

❦

Early Promise, Late Reward

"When the world is sick of many ills," Helen wrote in *Farewell Summer*, "the place to be in is the place where you belong; you will find reassurance there, in a tall tree, in the grass, a flower -- in the gentle contour of hills, pasture, and wood. 'As water to our thirst, so is the rock, the ground, to our eyes and hands and feet'."[1]

The Santmyers' home on Third Street had been sold out of the family, but Helen's brother-in-law, Fred Anderson, had arranged to buy the much-changed house back for them. While the Santmyers had been away, it had been made into a two-family house. The big side yard with the fountain had been sold and in its place was another house. The wrought iron fence had been removed and the garden had fallen into disrepair. It wasn't quite the house they had left only a few years before, still it was good to be home again!

The first item on the agenda, once they were ensconced, was to find a job for Helen. As luck would have it, Helen had a friend who worked in the Dayton Public Library, and Mildred Sandoe told her they had an opening for someone in the Reference Room. She was sure Helen could do the job. It was a librarian assistant's position and it didn't pay much, only $2600 a year, a considerable drop in pay from what Helen had been making as Dean of Women at Cedarville College.

Helen didn't want to work in a library, she didn't want to take a cut in pay, and at her age, with her educational background, she didn't want an assistant's job of any kind. But she had learned to settle for what she could get, and she needed a job in order to pay the bills. On August 20, 1953, Helen started a new career. She didn't consider it a career, however, it was just a means to an end when, in 1961, she could retire. In the meantime, as usual, she intended to do her best.

Before the new job started, however, Helen returned to Wellesley for her thirty-fifth reunion. It was a wonderful respite from her dreary life. In 1947 she had written for the *Purple Page*, "...in these decades life stands still and only time has wings."[2] By 1953, she echoed that melancholy sentiment. "...The middle aged disguise never replaces the reality of youth and long ago. The memories endure."[3] Reunion over, she returned to Xenia and her new position in Dayton.

Helen liked libraries and she had a friend there. It shouldn't be too bad, and she could drive back and forth with Mildred, after all. The job consisted of answering people's questions about three-quarters of the time. The rest of the job involved special assignments such as maintaining the Dayton Collection files or the Genealogy Collection, etc. Helen, with all of her early promise, worked at that job for seven years! On September 6, 1960, at age sixty-five, she retired to the rest of her life.

In October of 1954, not many months after they returned to Xenia, Mr. Santmyer died. A scant seven months later, April of 1955, Mrs. Santmyer joined him. Helen was alone now. She undertook the restoration of the family home, as near as possible, to the way she had remembered it. She even found an old iron fence to replace the original one that had been taken down. She restored the garden to its former glory and settled down with her dog to write.

But life is unpredictable. Sometimes it holds surprises. The first twist of fate involved Mildred Sandoe who was now commuting to her job in Cincinnati. The commute was long, and she complained about getting home so late. Because she often stopped at Helen's house on the way home for a drink or a late supper, it occurred to Helen that it would be simpler if Mildred sold her own house and moved into Helen's. She had plenty of room, after all, and they were compatible. Mildred could drive to work in the morning, and Helen would do her writing at home. It was agreed. As a result, Mildred became the catalyst that Helen needed for her writing.

While Mildred commuted to work Helen was busy. She had started work on a book about Xenia, several chapters of which she sent to *The Antioch Review* in nearby Yellow Springs. In January of 1956, the Chairman of the Editorial Board wrote to tell Miss Santmyer that they would like to publish three of them: *The Cemetary, There Were Fences* and *Four Corners*. With a few small revisions, they would like to publish one in their next issue. "...You will receive a small check and three (complimentary) copies of the issue in which your article appears."[4]

It was not until 1962 that Helen put the chapters together with others and sent the manuscript to Weldon Kefauver, then Director of The Ohio State University Press. "I realized with the very first paragraph that I had something extraordinary in my hands,"[5] he said, and, with the assistance of Dr. Arthur Schlesinger, arranged for *Ohio Town* to be selected for the fall list of OSU Press publications catalogue. The book was well received by local residents, but it only had moderate financial success until the rights were bought by Harper Row and re-published in 1984.

The publication of *Ohio Town* prompted an outpouring of sentiment: thanks, gratitude, and praise. Rachel Townsley, who lived in Cedarville and whose daughter, Doris, had been a student of Helen's, wrote, "I read [*Ohio Town*] fast for I couldn't wait to go slowly -- so I shall read it many times." She continued, "Everyone who reads it will be able to adapt it to their own town and experience. Greene Countians may enjoy it more than others, but it does have universal appeal..."[6]

Another enthusiastic reader wrote to tell her: "I have just finished reading the review copy of *Ohio Town*...The thing is that when the book arrived I thought I would just dip into it to see how OSU Press had handled the editing and make-up and found myself reading from cover to cover, charmed anew by a book I thought I was thoroughly familiar with."[7] As a busy editor, he said he had no higher praise!

From a classmate came a letter to Santy, her old college nickname "... you might be interested to know that H___ and I are on page 223 of *Ohio Town*" [referring to a high school play at the Opera House in which both ladies had been part of the cast]. They were pleased to have found themselves in the book, but, the friend continued, "H___ cannot equal my pride in a long standing association with and affection for the author!"[8]

The many letters of recognition and appreciation meant more to Helen than the money she would make. It had always been the fame that Helen sought -- to her that equaled success. [The archives at the OSU Library hold boxes of such letters to attest to that success.] Such comments as, "I am so grateful for your gift of expression...and sharing memories," and "...the philosophy which marks [*Ohio Town*'s] pages has put my own memories in perspective."[9] Helen had waited all of her life for recognition like this.

But there was more to come. Mildred Sandoe began to encourage Helen to dig out the manuscript she had worked on for years and prepare it for publication. Helen had written the saga longhand in many bound ledger books, and it needed to be typed on white paper and edited for it was much too long. When Weldon Kefauver heard that Helen was working on another book, he contacted her and asked to see it. Mildred stuck with Helen. Steady pressure from someone who cared was what Helen had needed. The Ohio State University Press agreed to publish the book Helen called "...*And Ladies of the Club*," but asked if she would cut the length of it.

Helen always had a problem with cutting her work. Even with Mildred's help she was reluctant to cut anything. "If they don't want to read it they can skip that part," she suggested. Weldon would request a deletion and Helen would say, "Put a checkmark in the margin and I'll think about it." Few deletions were accepted.

Finally, after much haggling, OSU Press agreed to publish a small quantity of the book. They only printed about a thousand copies and today those volumes are collectors' items. But the book was long and expensive, and OSU Press had little money to spend on publicizing it so it was not surprising that the book never reached mainstream America.

Again, fate took a surprising turn. As it happened, one of the few books published by OSU Press was read by a woman in Cleveland. She was enchanted with the book and sent it to her son, who was a television producer in California, declaring it was the best book she had read in years and it might be something he would consider producing. Things began to move quickly. The producer contacted a friend of his who happened to be with a large writers' agency in New York City; Weldon Kefauver was contacted about selling his rights for "...*And Ladies of the Club*" to Putnam, who would re-issue it. They flew out to discuss the matter with Helen, and the deal was consummated.

The literary world was stunned when the book written by a frail little old woman was selected as a Book-of-the-Month selection and became an instant best seller. A June 1984 headline read: "Her dream comes true...at the age of eighty-eight."[10] Helen, although suffering from emphysema, was in great demand by the press for interviews and sought after for television appearances on the *Tonight Show*, the *Today Show*, and countless other talk shows. Traveling, not by train as she had dreamed so many years ago, but by chauffeured limousines and airplanes.

"Too bad success didn't come sooner when she was younger,"[11] one reporter quipped. Helen laughed and replied that if it had she probably wouldn't have had all the publicity. Her greatest fear was that people would only remember how old she was and not the legacy of her writing.

Asked why she had written the book, Helen told them: "I wanted to show what life was like when people relied on themselves -- when they had principles."[12] One columnist for *Newsday* noted that Helen was dismayed because Americans seemed to be losing their self-reliance. She abhorred the socialism introduced by Roosevelt's New Deal, and she was irritated by Sinclair Lewis's cynical portrayal of the small town in his novel, *Main Street*."

That's part of the reason she wrote her book. She wanted her readers to know the other side of Lewis's *Main Street* and appreciate the fact that the Midwest was no longer considered a place between the two coasts. Helen, by her gifts of observation and communication, wanted to be our guide through her small town to give us an appreciation for the history behind it.

"I never dreamed anyone would be interested in the book or that it would be so popular...I still don't understand it. I guess it appeals to people who have lives like those in the book -- not very exciting."[13] But Helen's books made an impact because they projected the images of that time when manners and morals were the code of behavior. It was a gentler time, and one when people knew what was expected of them and relied more on themselves.

A reader from Nebraska spoke for many when she wrote to Helen to tell her: "I have just finished reading your "...And Ladies of the Club." It's the best book I have read in years! I have never before written a fan letter to an author, but felt I must express my pleasure in your wonderful novel. First of all, I appreciated being able to read a book without having my sensitivities assaulted with the vulgarity and downright pornography present in most of today's best sellers. But, most of all I felt it was very well written."[14]

With the new attention to *Ohio Town* and the publication of "...Ladies," the two early books of Helen's, published in the 1920s, were reissued. How did Helen react to all of this success which she had sought for so many years and which she thought had eluded her? She took the media attention with amusement. She was not fond of most of its representatives. And what about the money her books were making? At this late age, she shrugged it off and said, "Now, when I want something, I can buy it."[15]

As Helen's success arrived, her health failed and she often entered the nursing home for rest and care. By the time of the great media event, Helen was permanently ensconced in Hospitality East and her long-time friend, Mildred Sandoe, had joined her there. By 1985, Helen was content to lie on her bed, with the oxygen tank always at hand, and read, rest and visit with selected callers. In her youth she was filled with great promise; in mid-life she had, in her mind at least, succeeded only in going down to the depths of failure; but by the last years she achieved greater success than she had ever dreamed of and greater wealth than she could have imagined!

If Helen had won many millions in the lottery, the money would have not meant success to her. She had always written to please herself, and it was in her work that she felt satisfaction. She wanted recognition, however, and hoped publishers would buy her writing. If they did not, at least she knew she had written well. Haynes Johnson, reviewing Helen's book for the *Washington Post* said, "Failure did not seem to have been a bother to her. Even after the book was accepted for publication, after a lifetime of effort, she had demonstrated her freedom from the shameless kinds of self promotion and personal selling that afflict today's publishing marketplace."[16]

Helen Hooven Santmyer had shown early promise as a writer, she knew that herself. But the rewards had taken many years to be realized. She had worked a long time and endured many disappointments before she achieved those "desirable ends" she dreamed of as a child. Her success, however, was greater than she had ever imagined. Helen was sorry her father had not lived to see her succeed. He would have been very proud of her, at last.

Postscript

❧

During the media events that followed the success of "...*And Ladies of the Club,*" everyone rushed to Xenia to interview Helen Santmyer, the extraordinary old lady ·who took fifty years to write her great American novel. They all wrote what they knew of the small town girl who made good, most of it inaccurate, but none of them knew Helen at all. Helen was good at posing, she had done it all her life, and she showed all those strangers the "externals;" the "internals" were hidden in her enigmatic smiles and thoughtful pauses, for Helen was a very private person. She was bemused by all the attention, but her real concern was that they would not let her be remembered for her writing.

Helen worked at her craft and wrote from the heart. She desperately wanted to earn money, but she wrote for herself and hoped people would want to buy what she wrote. At the end of *Farewell Summer,* written when she had reached middle age, she said, "Solitary women like me...in every day and time...cling with all the strength of our memories to the old ways...who when they see the life they know not only doomed, but dead and nearly forgotten...sit down alone to write the elegies."[1]

During the times I came from Connecticut to visit with Helen at the nursing home in 1984, having no idea of writing her biography, she and I just talked. It was never an interview. We reminisced about women's clubs since my grandmother had been a founding member of the one in Cedarville, Cedarville as it had been in the 1930s, and the changing scene in Xenia and our country. I could not remember back as far as

Helen could for I was only a child when she taught in Cedarville, but we both agreed that what we had known was "not only doomed, but dead and very nearly forgotten."[2]

Outwardly, Helen was not the innocent country girl the media expected to find. The old lady smoked and drank straight bourbon and dressed in a somewhat exotic fashion, but inwardly she was not much changed from the young girl who wrote home so enthusiastically from Wellesley College many years before. She had traveled to Europe and had crossed this wide country many times. However, she did not write of those places, but rather of her own time and place where morality, hard work and independence were expected. She wrote with great love of the past and tried to share her love with those who would read.

People have asked me what I thought was the most memorable thing about Helen. Those who worked with her on the publishing of "...And Ladies of the Club" said it was her persistance and singlemindedness. But Helen was not persistant. She wrote because she was, above all, a writer and she wrote to please herself. It was Helen's friend who was persistant and singleminded in seeing Helen's book through completion. I believe the most memorable thing about Helen Santmyer was her ability to paint verbal pictures and communicate her ideas to her readers. In other words, her ability to write.

Appendix

"Helen Hooven Santmyer, 90, of the Hospitality Homes in Xenia, died in her sleep Friday, February 21, 1986. She had been in failing health for the past month. She was buried in a private graveside service on Saturday."[1]

Bibliography

INTRODUCTION

[1]Santmyer, Helen Hooven. "...*And Ladies of the Club*." Columbus: Ohio State University Press, 1982.

[2]Santmyer, Helen Hooven. *Herbs and Apples*. New York: St. Martin's Press, 1987.

[3]Santmyer, Helen Hooven. *Fierce Dispute*. New York: St. Martin's Press. 1987.

[4]Santmyer, Helen Hooven. *Farewell Summer*. New York: Harper and Row Publishers, 1988.

[5]Lewis, Sinclair. *Main Street*. New York: Penquin New American Library, 1974.

[6]Anderson, Sherwood. Winesburg, Ohio. New York: Penquin Classics, 1992.

[7]Santmyer, Helen Hooven. Childhood Journal 1907. Ohio State University Library.

PART I - CHAPTER 1

[1]Calkins, Dr. Raymond. Commencement Address Class of 1918. Wellesley College, June 14, 1918.

[2]Santmyer, Helen Hooven. *Ohio Town*. Columbus: Ohio State University Press, 1962. p. 235.

[3]Ibid., p. 245.

[4]Ibid., p. 243.

[5]Ibid., p. 244.

[6]Santmyer, Helen Hooven. *Herbs and Apples*. New York: St. Martin's Press, 1987. p. 2.

[7]Santmyer, Helen Hooven. *Ohio Town*. Columbus: Ohio State University Press, 1962. p.244.

[8]Santmyer, Helen Hooven. *Herbs and Apples*. New York: St. Martin's Press, 1987. p.2.

[9]Santmyer, Helen Hooven. *Ohio Town*. Colubus: Ohio State University Press, 1962. p. 247.

[10]Santmyer, Helen Hooven. *Herbs and Apples*. New York: St. Martin's Press, 1987. p. 3.

CHAPTER 2

[1]Santmyer, Helen Hooven. *Herbs and Apples*. New York: St. Martin's Press, 1987. p. 19.

[2]Santmyer, Helen Hooven. Childhood Journal 1907. Ohio State University Library.

[3]Santmyer, Helen Hooven. *Herbs and Apples*. New York: St. Martin's Press, 1987. p. 19.

[4]Ibid., p. 17.

CHAPTER 3

[1]Unless otherwise noted, the quotes in this chapter are taken from personal letters written from Wellesley College between 1914 and 1916.

CHAPTER 4

[1]Unless otherwise noted, the quotes in this chapter are taken from personal letters written from Wellesley College between 1916 and 1918.

CHAPTER 5

[1]Unless otherwise noted, the quotes in this chapter are taken from personal letters written from Boston between 1918 and 1919.

CHAPTER 6

[1]Unless otherwise noted, the quotes in this chapter are taken from personal letters written from New York City between 1919 and 1921.

CHAPTER 7

[1]Unless otherwise noted, the quotes in this chapter are taken from personal letters written from Wellesley College between 1922 and 1923.

CHAPTER 8

[1]Unless otherwise noted, the quotes in this chapter are taken from personal letters written from the USS Montcalm and London, England during 1924.

CHAPTER 9

[1]Unless otherwise noted, the quotes in this chapter are taken from personal letters written from Oxford and London, England during 1924.

CHAPTER 10

[1]Unless otherwise noted, the quotes in this chapter are taken from personal letters written from Paris, France during 1924.

CHAPTER 11

[1]Unless otherwise noted, the quotes in this chapter are taken from personal letters written from Oxford and the English countryside during 1925.

[2]Reeve, Clare. *Progress of Romance*. Published in England; out of print.

[3]Review of *Herbs and Apples*, Anniston Star, Alabama, 1985.

CHAPTER 12

[1]Unless otherwise noted, the quotes in this chapter are taken from personal letters written from London, England during 1925.

CHAPTER 13

[1]Unless otherwise noted, the quotes in this chapter are taken from personal letters written from Oxford and London, England during 1926.

CHAPTER 14

[1]Unless otherwise noted, the quotes in this chapter are taken from personal letters written from the MacDowell Colony, Peterborough, New Hampshire in 1930.

CHAPTER 15

Letter from *Atlantic Monthly*.

CHAPTER 16

[1]Santmyer, Helen Hooven. *Farewell Summer*. New York: Harper & Row Publishers, 1988.

[2]Wellesley College's *Purple Rage*. Class of 1918 Alumnae News, 1947.

[3]Ibid., 1951.

[4]Santmyer, Helen Hooven. *Ohio Town*. Columbus: Ohio University Press, 1962.

[5]Letter from Chairman of the Education Board, Yellow Springs, *Antioch Review*, 1956.

[6]Letter from Weldon Kefauver, Director, Ohio State University Press, 1962.

[7]Johnson, Haynes. Washington, D.C.: *Washington Post*, 1985.

APPENDIX

[1]Obituary, *Xenia Gazette*, February 21, 1986.

Joyce Crosby Quay (signature)

Early Promise, Late Reward

A Biography of Helen Hooven Santmyer

Author of "...And Ladies of the Club."

By Joyce Crosby Quay

Cover Design: Gil Fahey
Text Design: Robin McArdle

Copyright © 1995 by Joyce C. Quay

All rights reserved. No part of this book may be used or
reproduced in any manner without written permission,
except in the case of brief quotations embodied in critical
articles and reviews.

Library of Congress Cataloging in Publication Data

Quay, Joyce Crosby.
    Early promise, late reward: a biography of Helen Hooven Santmyer,
    author of "...And ladies of the night / by Joyce Crosby Quay.
        p.   cm.
    Includes bibliographical references (p. 131).

        1. Santmyer, Helen Hooven, 1895- --Biography.   2. Women novelists,
    American--20th century--Biography.   3. Xenia (Ohio)--Social life and
    customs.   4. Xenia (Ohio)--Biography.   I. Title.
    PS3537.A775Z84   1995
    813'.52--dc20
    [B]   94-46813
                                                                           CIP

First Published in 1995 by:
Knowledge, Ideas & Trends, Inc.
1131-0 Tolland Turnpike, Suite 175
Manchester, CT 06040
Telephone: 1-800-826-0529

ISBN 1-879198-15-0

10 9 8 7 6 5 4 3 2 1

Printed in the United States of America